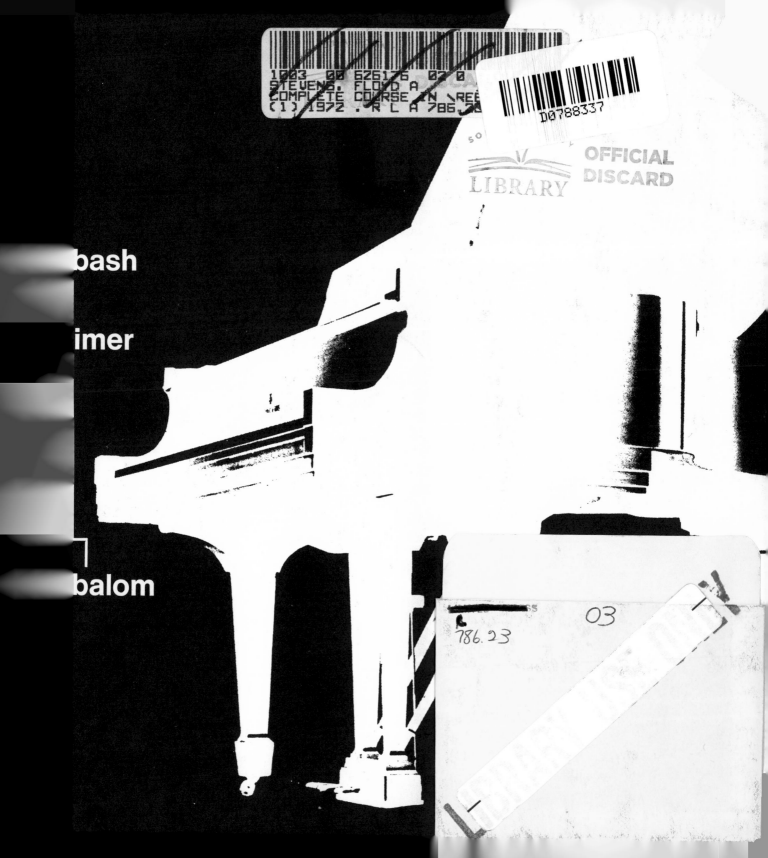

bash

imer

balom

Complete Course in
Professional Piano Tuning, Repair, and Rebuilding

Complete course in professional

Piano Tuning, Repair,

and Rebuilding

Floyd A. Stevens, Ph.D.

Professional / Technical Series

 Nelson-Hall Publishers
Chicago

ISBN 911012-07-9

Library of Congress Catalog Card No. 74-173598

Copyright © 1972 by Floyd A. Stevens

Third Printing, 1982

Manufactured in the United States of America

10   9   8   7   6   5   4   3

The paper in this book is pH neutral (acid-free).

To Kent, my six-year-old apprentice,
who is learning to break strings
with the best of them.

Contents

Illustrations

Diagrams

Publisher's Foreword

This book is a nontechnical presentation of piano tuning, repairing, and rebuilding techniques. It also offers instruction in tuning and repairing electronic organs and pianos.

The instruction is practical and written in simple English. Technical terms are used only when no satisfactory common synonyms are available, but these should present no problem. Schematic diagrams identify components and clarify functions to make understanding complete.

The short cuts for getting jobs done have been tested and proven. Obviously, these help get work done faster and more efficiently. Furthermore, only such instruction which a technician needs is included. There are no explanations of theory, since none are needed.

It is probable that many of the techniques you will learn are being revealed publicly for the first time. This is not because they are new, but because it is not customary for craftsmen to reveal their secrets.

The instruction is based on an extensive background of college training in music, careful experimentation, and 15 years of practical experience as a craftsman. The author has tuned pianos in homes, for dealers, and in concert halls for the most discriminating and critical artists. He also has appeared on television as a musical performer, and otherwise worked with musicians most of his career.

His experience in tuning, rebuilding, and restyling pianos from the smallest consoles through the largest grands has convinced him that the profession is not only financially rewarding but emotionally satisfying. Technicians and tuners enjoy independence, unusually stable earnings, and security because they fulfill a need. As may be expected, the demand for tuners is great, and not nearly enough men and women are training to meet it.

The novice in the art of piano tuning should find this book indispensable. The piano owner who wants to keep his piano in tune will discover that this book is easy to understand. Even the professional can learn much from the pages that follow. He will recognize that, for the first time, the complete range of piano tuning techniques is presented in compact form in one volume.

Acknowledgments

The valuable help of many individuals and firms made this book possible. It could not have been done without them. My special thanks to the Baldwin Piano Company of Cincinnati, Ohio, who granted permission to reprint much of the instruction which appears in Lessons 3, 4, and 14, as well as many diagrams, and Willard Simms of that company who did exhaustive research and supplied a considerable amount of invaluable information; the Conn Corporation of Oak Brook, Illinois, who granted permission to reprint much of the material in Lesson 7; Kenneth Caddell, who read the manuscript and made many constructive suggestions; Joseph Glover and Dennis Woodall, who provided good counsel and the inspiration for this project; James H. Burton, editor of *Piano Technician's Journal*, who encouraged the writing of the book and furnished valuable diagrams; C. D. Goosen, who did the photography; and finally my wife, Opal, and my son, Bruce, who helped with editing and gave encouragement when seemingly insurmountable obstacles appeared.

Introduction

The piano is unique among musical instruments of the world. It has universal acceptance, prestige, and an infinite capacity for delivering glorious musical sounds. Next to the guitar, it is the most popular instrument in use.

With the possible exception of the organ, only the piano is truly self-supporting as an instrument. It demands all the ability that a pair of talented hands can supply; furthermore, the artist must have dexterous fingers to match his creativity and interpretiveness. The piano, too, is more than adequate to respond to the full efforts of two pianists playing simultaneously on its keyboard.

That the piano is the choice of many renowned artists is well known. But its use has not been confined to classical compositions. For decades, especially in America, popular artists have offered so-called ''standard'' songs. Today, the piano is coming to the front strongly as an instrument that gives force and clarity to the most modern of musical forms, including those devised by youthful entertainers.

The piano is heard frequently on records, in concert halls, at festivals, and on television and radio. This is so because the piano interprets a vast range of musical forms, and expresses the complete harmonic structure, figuration, and dynamic range of a composition.

The author recalls his boyhood days when he attended concerts and listened to some of the great vocalists giving forth their art, always with the able assistance of the accompanying artist in the background. However, most children received their introduction to music by becoming piano students, either willingly or with the gentle prodding of parents. Learning to play is not the chore it once was, thanks to the enlightened instruction now available.

No longer do piano teachers insist that pupils plod through endless hours of scale practice. Finger exercises are futile and a thing of the past. At last, teachers understand that in the music itself will be found precisely the difficulties to be mastered. Today, young people, and those not so young, are finding that piano study is an absorbing and useful way to express the songs which they find haunting their memories. This development should spur greater interest and attract new flocks of eager beginners.

Basically, the piano is a combination of harp strings and a percussive keyboard system borrowed from the early organ. The first designs encompassed a few strings serving a number of notes (much like the guitar, in that fretting or movable bridges were necessary). Then the number of strings was increased and the keyboard dulcimer developed. This instrument was referred to as the clavicymbal or clavecin, and in English, as the harpsichord. Refinements were made, and soon there was a single string for each tone. The instrument so constructed was known as the "couched harp" (a harp enclosed in an energy box), or spinet. Strings were plucked by a quill attached to the end of a wooden "jack." While this development allowed for much more musical scope, there was still no means for reducing the tone from loud to soft.

There was a dramatic change in 1711 when Christofori invented a hammer mechanism. This system and its mechanism, because of the ability inherent in its escapement to produce a force, either hard or soft, which could be altered to any degree in between the two extremes, he called pianoforte (piano, meaning soft; forte, meaning loud). Subsequent refinements of the mechanism led to the development of what we now know as the piano.

With sustaining pedal, selective sustain, and soft pedal, the piano is truly a remarkable and versatile instrument. It has from 6,000 to 12,000 parts, depending on the model, assembled into a marvelous, melodious musical device.

Pianos come in different sizes and configurations. At the top of the list stands the concert grand, which, in its present form, represents the highest skills of the pianomaker's art. Its long speaking strings, made resonant by means of cleverly designed bearing points and masterfully designed bridges, energize a delicately crowned sound board, and produce tones which are clearer at 60 feet than near the piano. No concert hall is too large for one of these instruments to master, especially when thrust into vibrant life by a fine pianist. No whisper of love is softer than the diminuendo of which a well-designed concert grand is capable. Nine feet of piano can be played as softly as the breath of morning mist, or as loudly as the crash of cymbals. Here is an instrument with two claims upon the heart: the magnificence of its cabinetry and line, and the sonorous grandeur of its tone.

Scaled down from this monstrous beauty are the seven-, six-, and five-foot grands. Though unable to resound with the great voice of the concert grand, these smaller grands are capable of great magnificence of tone and deep beauty of expression when well designed and carefully constructed. The repeating action housed within their bodies is equal in most instances to that of the large grands; thus, the limitation of space which has curtailed their volume and power has not necessarily interfered with their ability to faithfully project every nuance of feeling and expression which the pianist can "touch into" the instrument. They reward the master, but not as loudly. They can expose the charlatan and reveal the difference between a piano player and an artist.

Not to be overlooked is the old upright. Many of the earlier uprights include in their design all the speaking power of the medium-sized grands. Only the way in which they have been styled to fit against the wall is different, insofar as tonal quality is concerned. But, alas, the mechanism which moves the hammer is altered, necessarily, from that of the grand.

The trilling repetition on most uprights is not as rapid nor effortless as in the grand. Given this one slight flaw, the upright, when well designed and made, will deliver more music than most people have technique to attempt. After all, the older, larger uprights have the same sound-board area as medium-sized grands. Their strings and bridges are often designed to operate as well. Only the action is less responsive, in most cases. (There are uprights being made today which incorporate sensitive actions, and there is at least one which offers a key response that allows the pianist to perform at the last one-third of the travel of the key when depressed.) The scale design, with its even flow of tonality throughout the tenor and treble, and with no break in its structure, offers sounds better than any number of medium-sized grand pianos on the market today. So, the day of the upright is not over, nor is the upright less valuable than the grand in every case.

Modern living is beginning to include some of the things which make living more pleasant and meaningful. Music is one of these things, and we are beginning to make room for musical instruments. But, for some time, space has been at a premium in most homes. Designed to meet this condition, the spinet, small console, and drop action pianos have kept the piano business very much alive for the last few decades.

Spinets do not have the sounding area of uprights or grands. Therefore, they do not give out, in the average case, the volume of the other pianos. They also are restrictive as to string lengths, which means that the bass will have to be less resonant and long sounding than the bass found in larger pianos. However, whenever a spinet is made without skimping on the quality of the materials, and the men who construct it care about making an instrument with beauty of tone, it can be a very good piano indeed.

Actions in spinets can be equal to the best of the uprights, and often are. The author has tuned spinets which feature actions surpassing medium grands in their responsiveness. Such spinets have scales designed by people who are concerned about the piano as an instrument, and who do not look at it as a piece of furniture to sell. The spinet, then, can provide more than a satisfactory playing experience. It also can be beautifully played. But, there is nothing shoddier, in sound and appearance, than a cheap spinet.

No piano, whether the largest grand or the smallest spinet, is any good without regular service and care. First of all, pianos go out of tune with great frequency. They are made in such a way that all the parts of the sounding system work together, but when any one of these components changes, the tune of the piano changes.

The strings are under great tension, and the tuning pins may turn in their holes as these tensions equalize themselves over the length of the string. This puts the unisons out of tune. The temperature and humidity of a room may change. This means that the strings will expand or contract due to temperature changes, and the sound board with its supported bridges will grow with humidity and shrink slightly with dryness. This causes a change in the stresses upon the strings, and the piano goes out of tune.

Generally, competent manufacturers agree that a piano should be tuned no less than twice a year and would be better served if tuned more frequently. Pianos used constantly should be tuned monthly, or weekly, depending on the use they are put to. Delaying the tuning of a piano is no way to save money. First of all, the piano is designed so that all parts are stressed properly when it is in tune. This means that an out-of-tune piano has unusual stresses occurring at points within the framework. The result of these nondesigned stresses can range from splitting of the sound board to loosening of the bridges. In addition, the curvature of the board is designed to sound properly when the piano is in tune.

Pianos not only have poor sound when they are out of tune, but they sound less musical because the sound board is not functioning as it was designed. When, after long delay, the technician-tuner is asked to put a piano in proper tune, he will, if he is honest, advise that it needs to be tuned several times in order to stay in tune, since the strings and board have been sagging too long. Furthermore, the charge to get it to stay in tune will about equal the total expense of having had it tuned at six-month intervals.

We live in a land of varying climatic conditions. Pianos swell and expand in the Northwest but dry out and crack in the Southwest. In the Midwest, the changes from high to low humidity can cause both effects. Remember, a piano is made of wood. Almost everything in it is made of wood. What isn't made of wood depends on wooden parts to make it work.

Even the best-processed wood swells with high humidity and shrinks with dryness. Thus, pianos tuned to A-440 in a dry climate will rise in pitch and go out of tune as soon as the humidity rises significantly.

Winter heating in a home will cause pianos, tuned to proper pitch, to dry out and sink in pitch throughout the center section of the piano. This puts the piano out of tune. Generally speaking, pianos which are kept anywhere in this country will go up and down in pitch as the humidity rises and falls. Thus a piano in Oregon, when tuned to pitch in normal humidity for that region, will fall in pitch when dryness occurs and become sharp in pitch when humidity rises.

The author is acquainted with one small manufacturer who moved his piano-constructing business to Utah. He reasoned that no matter where he shipped his pianos, they would swell and get tighter than usual, since most other places in America were damper than Utah.

Every real change of weather develops business for you in piano service. This is one of the better reasons for becoming a technician and tuner. Pianos need to be tuned often!

An even better reason for becoming a craftsman in piano technology is that, behind every artist on the concert stage, there is an unseen artist. He's the tuner-technician. Also, students play better when the piano is properly tuned. The action works more smoothly and the family is happier. Teachers teach more efficiently when an A is an A.

There are few genuine crafts remaining in our mechanized world. Not many offer opportunities for splendid, appreciated craftsmanship. Piano servicing is one of these. It practically guarantees a rare kind of security. To do a thing well, and to be aware of your skill, earns genuine respect from your peers, and gives you a feeling of accomplishment. Too many enterprises today depend on a fabricated demand which too often has been related to need. Piano service is real. There is a need for it. Pianos need care on a continuing basis.

One can learn this profession and practice it constructively. Not many occupations offer that benefit. For those who love craftsmanship for its own sake, piano tuning is a natural. To the man who wonders what his destiny is, piano tuning holds out a new life. However, like anything else that is good, the mastery of piano tuning must be paid for in advance; the bad can be paid for afterwards. It takes time to learn the simple rules which make this profession unlike any other; it takes effort to put the principles into practice and become adept at using them. But, once mastered, your skill is yours always. Nothing can take it away. You develop talent which few possess and fewer still understand.

Someone once asked me, "What makes a good piano tuner?" After some thought, I came to the conclusion that the vision of craftsmanship is what makes a good piano tuner. It isn't charm, or college degrees, or certificates, or the right connections that make a qualified craftsman. Only a vision in a man's mind of himself as a craftsman and an excellent practitioner of his skill will do it!

There are people who possess degrees and certificates to prove that they are one thing or another. Unfortunately, we often find that they are not what the certificates say, because they can't do what the certificates claim they can do. Or at least, they can't do well what they are supposed to do. Piano technology has only one aristocracy, and that is the aristocracy of achievement! Either you can tune, or you're not considered to be a piano tuner. Your competence, or lack of it, will be revealed as soon as someone sits down to play a piano that you have just tuned. That is the moment of truth!

The tools of piano technology, as described in this book, are designed for a special purpose, and are not particularly expensive. Many tuners say that the ownership of these tools is especially rewarding; the tools we use are unique to our profession, and in many cases, their nomenclature sets us apart from ordinary skilled men. Chromed and shiny, these tools will enable you to make your dream of financial independence a reality.

The fees charged by competent craftsmen are equal to those in the professions. Wisely conserved, the yearly income of the average craftsman enables him to have a good home in a nice neighborhood, to buy a new car every other year, and to take a vacation abroad. He is no man's servant (unless he wants to be). And this profession is ideally suited for those who want a business of their own.

The craft of piano technology knows no limitation of age or sex. Perhaps the best piano technicians are those who have learned their craft early and have matured into extremely competent tuners and rebuilders. However, some people do not mellow with age, for experience alone is not a good teacher. Active practice and constant, thoughtful concentration on the principles which make this a craft will help the student outdistance the man who relies solely on doing the same thing over and over in the same old way. That is why a person who goes into this line of work can become one of the best craftsmen if he chooses, without waiting for 30 years of experience. Some have only one year's experience, which unfortunately they have repeated 30 times. Others, in a few years, become extraordinary.

One of the better craftsmen, who is known well in the field for his fine tuning in movie studios on the West Coast, spent many years as a musician and arranger before deciding to make piano technology his life's work. He has crowned his career with glory and respect, even though he did not begin in a piano factory in the old days and work his way up to be a fine tuner. Age is no deterrent. A fresh and creative point of view may often be found in a mellowed head and be absent in a youthful one.

Women thrive in this craft, as in other occupations. They do well in tuning if they apply the same creativity as they do elsewhere. The author has attended meetings where women tuners were pointed to with pride and discussed with respect for their abilities. Tuning requires little physical strength. There are no requirements of manual dexterity which might exceed a woman's capability. In fact, it is obvious in some cases that women could do this painstaking regulating work more acceptably than men. The author has small fingers and only normal strength and finds the work somewhat easier because of this. Tuning should be a rewarding field for a woman if she will be precise. There is no apparent discrimination due to race or color. After all, this is an independent business. The technician is usually self-employed.

Special aptitudes, such as musical talent and related abilities, are not required to do things which a piano tuner does. We do not tune by musical notation, but by beats within the temperament and octave intervals of the piano. In some cases, it is possible that a highly developed musical background could be a handicap. This would be especially true if the erstwhile musician were to try to tune with musicality as his guide in setting temperament. It cannot be done accurately time after time this way.

Of course, it would be gratifying if the author could say that piano tuning is extremely easy to learn and requires very little time or concentration. But this cannot be said with truth. This is not a book on how to learn piano tuning in one evening. However, it is a book which explains simple, practical skills which anyone can master with a reasonable amount of practice. By applying the simple and concise instructions in this book, you can become a good piano technician and tuner. With more practice and concentration, you can become expert.

When people have confidence in your ability to practice this art, they will request your services. There are few other businesses which offer more to the man or woman who satisfies a client. Good piano tuners are hard to find.

Piano tuning is the key which opens doors to homes of the musically cultured and financially able. You will enter those homes as a qualified craftsman who renders a valuable service. People will respect your skill, once you master it well enough to respect it yourself. With the men and women who work in this field, you will share secret knowledge and a fine sense of self-worth. Money will follow as surely as night follows day. But first you must see yourself as a piano tuner, and approach the art with a vision of craftsmanship.

Lesson 1 Let's look at the piano

The piano, as it has evolved to the present day, is an imposing instrument. The number of parts will range from approximately 6,000 to 12,000. Physically, the total stored energy within its strings and face frame will approach the equivalent of 20 tons and may go higher in pianos with laminated sound boards. Probably no other instrument in the world has made so many musicians its slave and been so universally taught to persons from 2 to 92. Over the years, many new inventions have been offered, and claims have been made that they would supplant this instrument. But the piano remains, and probably will always remain, a basic tool for music and the companion of the musically great.

Tuners, in discussions among themselves, may say that one manufacturer's product stands out above the others, depending, of course, upon the experience each tuner has had with a particular brand. There are differences in pianos. The acoustic value of different types of cases, the methods used to prepare the working parts at the factories, and the stringing scale design make for many variations. But the one basic difference often overlooked is the attitude of the technician who prepares the piano for the home or for the performing artist.

As a matter of policy, no company would offer on today's market an instrument which it knew had less value than that offered by a competitor at the same price. For the sake of becoming competent and doing his best work, the tuner-technician should view each product as being the result of the best application of money and materials a particular company can devise. No designer would intentionally come up with a string scale that was defective. Nor would an action-maker seek to make a sluggish action. *It is the responsibility of the man or woman who holds the title of tuner-technician to get the most satisfactory results out of a particular instrument that his skill and attention can produce.*

Some pianos may be better than others. But all pianos can be made to give forth their best. And a relatively old piano (or perhaps an inexpensive, new piano) which is regulated properly and tuned to its peak will usually be a finer performing piano than any instrument — no matter how new or expensive — to which the craftsman has not given his maximum effort.

The major parts of a piano

The major parts of a piano obviously have names. These names should be committed to memory. You will use them all your life in the piano business.

All pianos are built in substantially the same way. The upright has the same construction features as the smaller spinet, and the grand is basically the same as an upright lying on its back. Building a piano consists of making a strong back, either with large back posts of wood, or, as in some English pianos, casting a heavy iron rim around the perimeter of the cast iron plate. One of these two methods is necessary in order to take the strain of the 18 to 22 tons of pressure which the strings exert when the piano is tuned to concert pitch of 440 cycles per second on A.

After the back is made, the sound board is placed from edge to edge (side to side) and from the bottom to slightly below the top of the back frame. The sound board is usually made of close-grained spruce. It is chosen for the number of its uniformly-spaced rings per inch and air dried for some years prior to being kiln dried. The sound board is crowned, or curved upward in the center, somewhat in the manner of a violin face, and held in this configuration by ribs, which are glued to its back. Above the sound board is placed the wrest plank or pin block, which extends from side to side at the top of the piano. The pin block is usually made of laminated hardwoods, so designed that the tuning pins, which enter it from the front, contact the greatest number of possible end grains as they pierce it.

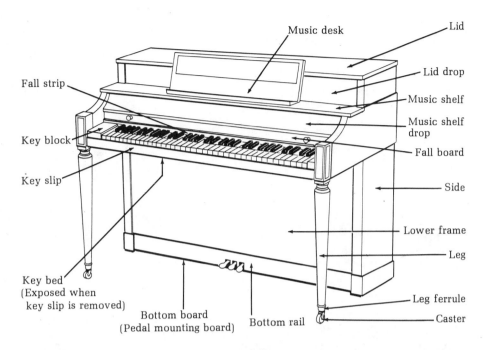

SPINET AND CONSOLE CASE PARTS

Over the back, thus far assembled, is placed the cast iron plate, which is basically a harp. It is fastened to the back with bolts which pass through the pin block and sound board. At the upper edge of the cast iron plate, there are either cast or drilled 230 to 251 tuning pin holes, which accept the tuning pins. Pilot holes are drilled into the wrest plank, and in many factories, the tuning pins are driven into these holes with a two-pound hammer.

For the benefit of the student, and for the advanced technician as well, it might be a good idea for us to think for a moment why the components just mentioned were made as they were. Much of the trouble in piano repair, and no little amount of the difficulties some men experience in sound tuning, can be eliminated by thinking about the functions of these units. A sound board is crowned because the resonance inherent in the close-grained wood is enhanced by the crowning, which induces a tension into all the layers as they press against each other. In designing the piano, the scale is laid out so that full advantage of the inherent resonance qualities of the sound board will be taken. If you take a good look at a violin, you will see that the

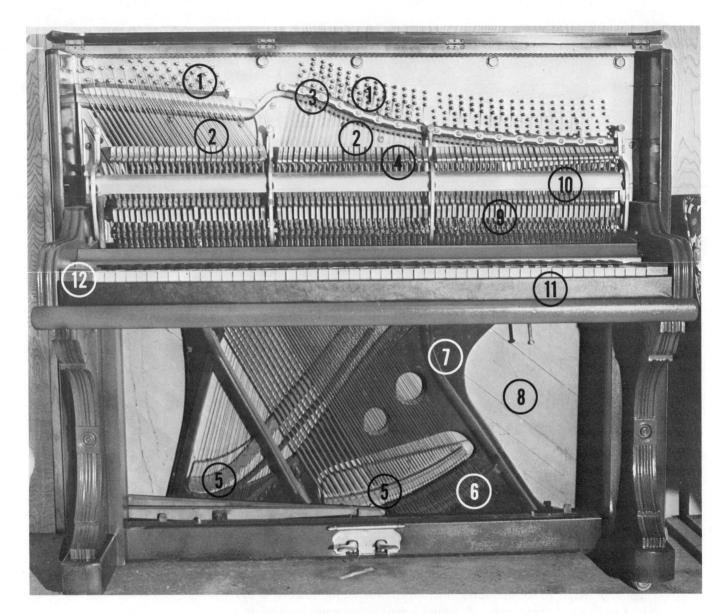

Front view of an upright piano with the boards removed, and the inner construction revealed.

1 tuning pins	5 bridges	9 back checks
2 strings	6 hitch pins	10 hammer rail
3 capo or bearing bar	7 plate	11 key slip
4 hammers	8 sound board	12 key block

raised center section offers maximum resonance for vibrations from the strings when transmitted through the bridge to the box.

Unlike some other instruments, the piano has the bridge (either bass or treble) fastened by adhesives or in some other permanent manner to the resonating sound board. Obviously, as one tightens the strings which exert a downward pressure (called down bearing) on the bridge, movement of the crown of the sound board will occur. This may be quite small in a guitar or violin, but in a piano, with hundreds of strings pressing downward along the bridges and exerting seven pounds or thereabouts each in pressure on the sound board, the tension in one part of the sound board will change as strings are pulled up in a totally different part.

In pianos which are manufactured with a sound board made of laminated wood, a greater degree of tension will be required on each string, and a stronger downward pressure will be needed to produce full resonance. Also, the tuning will shift more obviously if these facts are not taken into account and soon will give rise to complaints that "the piano doesn't hold its tune."

The cast iron plate

The cast iron plate is made of cast iron because the resonance factor is quite low in this material. This is to avoid sympathetic, untunable vibrations in the speaking piano. Unfortunately, this also means that we are working with a material which does not weld satisfactorily. It is also subject to great strain in a piano and will crack if tensions are not properly applied or allowed to twist or otherwise deform the cast metal. Usually, a manufacturer will provide specifications for the cast iron plate which will allow at least 50% greater tension than should usually be required to put the piano in tune. Whatever the tolerance of overstrain provided, it has happened that foundries which are casting the plates have skimped on metal content; and just a few pounds less cast iron in critical spots can produce an "exploding plate."

Tuning a piano without proper checking of the bolts which hold the plate to the back or frame may not always lead to a broken plate, but will certainly lead to a highly unstable tuning if any bolts are loose. After all, these fasteners are seated in wood, and wood changes its density constantly with the changes in atmospheric conditions and fluctuations in humidity. Should the plate be improperly seated and held down, warpage can occur. The result may range from drifting

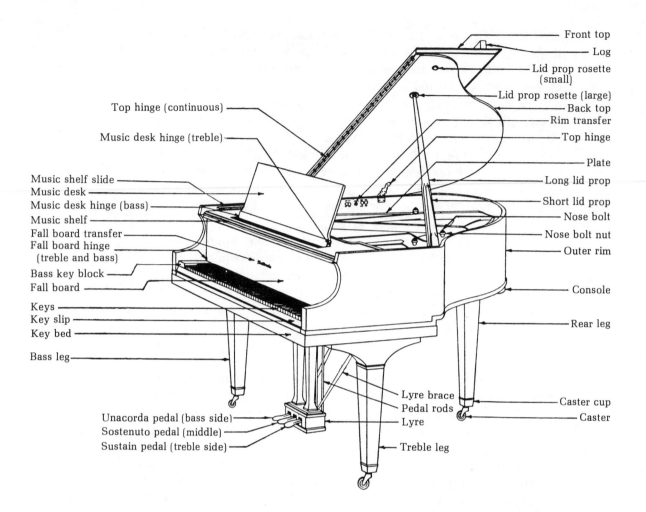

Front top
Log
Lid prop rosette (small)
Lid prop rosette (large)
Back top
Rim transfer
Top hinge
Plate
Long lid prop
Short lid prop
Nose bolt
Nose bolt nut
Outer rim
Console
Rear leg
Caster cup
Caster

Top hinge (continuous)
Music desk hinge (treble)
Music shelf slide
Music desk
Music desk hinge (bass)
Music shelf
Fall board transfer
Fall board hinge (treble and bass)
Bass key block
Fall board
Keys
Key slip
Key bed
Bass leg
Lyre brace
Pedal rods
Lyre
Unacorda pedal (bass side)
Sostenuto pedal (middle)
Sustain pedal (treble side)
Treble leg

BALDWIN GRAND PIANO CASE PARTS

tunability to complete fracture of the cast metal. If a plate is broken, it is best to replace it; but it can be repaired with metal plates bolted into the metal. Welding changes content and is not usually indicated.

Now, if you combine a piano scale using a laminated sound board, with its necessity of some additional tons of pressure upon the plate, and a cast iron plate, which is just a few pounds lighter than specified, or is not securely torqued down by the tuner, you have what might be called an explosive situation.

As the tuner (either in the store or in the home), you are the expert who can forestall much that could go wrong. You can make sure the plate is bedded tightly. You can place the tension evenly during tuning. The plate still might break. But if it does, you will know you did not contribute to its breakage. Hopefully, both the music dealer and the customer will know it, too.

As mentioned before, the bridges are fixed immovably to the sound board. These bridges are made of hardwood and are capped with a graphite surface. The lubrication is placed upon the bridge cap so that the strings which cross over the bridge will not stick to the wood during tuning. As the strings pass from the small hitch pin which is inserted in the lower rim of the cast iron plate, they come up over the bridge (which is slightly higher than the level of the string) and then continue upward to the bearing bar, and under the capo d'astro bar, thence onward to the tuning pin.

Bridges

In some pianos the bearing bar and capo bar and their tensioning arrangement are superceded by an agraffe. An agraffe is a small metal unit with reamed holes to accommodate the passage of a piano string. Upward tension from the agraffe to the tuning pin offers similar control of the string as results from the bearing bar and capo bar. As the string comes over the bridge, it is level, but upon being brought over the bearing bar and under the capo bar, the running level of the string is altered in such a way as to cause down-bearing upon the surface of the bridge.

In addition, through the use of two bridge pins, the string is caused to stagger slightly as it crosses the bridge. This gives a result which is called side-bearing. The strings are aligned properly in relation to other strings which pass over the bridge. At the tuning pin, the string is wrapped around three times. The friction that results when the tuning pin compresses fibers within the pin block causes the pin to stay about where it is put.

You probably noticed the statement: "the pin stays about where it is put." On some new pianos with extremely tight pin blocks, it seems to the experienced tuner that the pin stays just where it was put at the factory. Those who tune under the assumption that tuning takes place by turning the tuning pins may have problems. And further thought about the layout of a typical piano string, as it proceeds from hitch pin to tuning pin, might lead one to conclude that the *string* is what needs to be tuned, and that the tuning pin is just one part of the system.

Let us consider the segment of string between hitch pin and bridge. Surely, when the string is pulled to its specified tension at the distant end from the hitch pin, the small segment of string between hitch pin and bridge is likely to be under a slightly different tension than the longer part of the string between bridge and bearing bar or agraffe.

Now consider the small segment of string between upper bearing bar or agraffe and tuning pin. One might safely conclude that the small segment of string between these two points is likely to be under different tension than the long portion between the bridge and bearing bar. In fact, the design of string travel is such that it would seem impossible for the tension to be equal between these different points.

The sound and tune   The sound of a piano depends upon the vibrations of the speaking length of the string being transmitted through the bridge to the sound board, which in turn moves the air so that sound arrives at the human ear. *The tune of a piano depends upon equalizing the distinctly different portions of a piano string so that tensions are left nearly in balance, or if not, are regulated so that the speaking length will not be materially altered by the playing of the piano or other factors after tuning.*

Up to this point, we have considered the strange and shifting effects of uneven tensions applied to the sound board during tuning, and the vagaries which can occur as the result of upper plate wobble. The tuner and technician must know that, having minimized these variables, he can control the intricacies of piano wire as it courses on its way from hitch pin to tuning pin and excites the bridges.

There are ways to have control of this extremely variable component of the piano. Perfecting these ways means perfecting your tuning. And fine tuning depends upon constant consideration of the factors which, taken all together, can work with the tuner or against him. Trying to work intelligently with the components that are built into a piano can make all the difference. This is the way to make every piano sound its best. Not only does "the tuner alone preserve the tone," he usually improves it!

For the beginner, we will mention other parts of the piano which have nothing to do with the tuning. These are: the music shelf, which

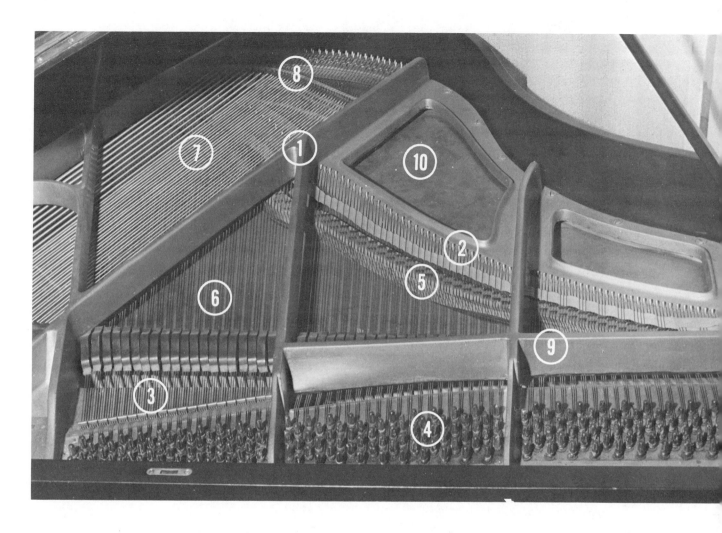

Interior view of a grand piano from the front. Note that the layout and basic structure are similar to that of the upright and spinet.

1 plate
2 hitch pins
3 agraffes
4 tuning pins
5 treble bridge
6 dampers

7 bass strings
8 bass bridge
9 bearing bar (integral with the plate)
10 sound board

Hammers can be seen underneath the lower treble strings.

supports the music; the fall board, which folds down or slides out to cover the keys; the name board; and the flange board, which is felted and lies across the top surface at the rear of the keys. At both ends of the keyboard are large wooden blocks called key blocks. The key slip is the small wooden strip in front of the lower surface of the keys. All of these parts are shown in photographs and diagrams in this lesson.

At this point, it would be a good idea for the beginning tuner to consider getting a piano to work with. Perhaps you can borrow or buy one from a relative or friend. If not, the purchase of an older piano would be a profitable investment. Older pianos are not costly, and often can be obtained just for moving them away. You will have a piano to practice on. Also, the repairing you do will make the instrument worth a great deal more than it was worth when you first got it. By applying what you learn from this book, you should be able to complete an instrument which can be sold for a tidy profit. Whether the piano you get is an upright, spinet, or grand, you will find many areas of similar construction and general design; thus, a technique used on one style can often be used to good advantage on another.

Get a clock! Most inexpensive clocks beat loudly, but find one that beats about two times per second. Move the slow-fast indicator until the ticking may be heard exactly two times per second. Keep the clock ticking beside you as you read. You won't need to concentrate on the ticking, but you will build up a sense of how long a second is. You will be using the time interval of one second all the time you tune pianos! So, get a clock, and keep it near.

An overall inspection of your piano prior to tuning

Look at the tuning pins. They may be rusty if the piano is old and sometimes if it is not old. They can be cleaned with a wire bristle brush or with a patented tuning-pin cleaning device which piano supply houses sell. The pins can be reblued with tuning pin bluing or a gun bluing stick (felt tipped), but be careful not to touch or damage the strings. *Keep oil or lubricants away from the strings, pin block, and tuning pins!* Do nothing which will adversely affect the friction between tuning pins and pin block.

Place the tuning hammer on the pins. At first, just one or two pins in each section will do. Using a tuning lever 10 in. in length from end to tip, you should exert about 20 pounds of pressure to move the

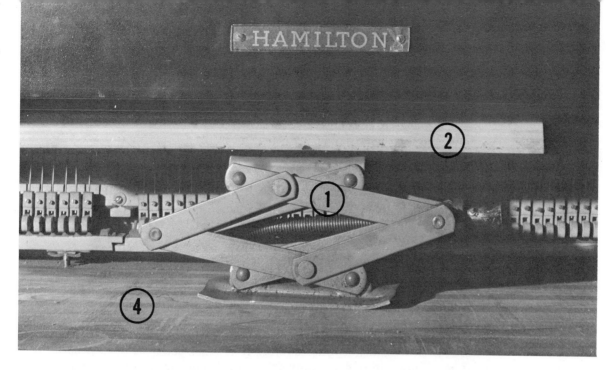

A scissors jack is used by the author for rebuilding and for block-ing up when any work is to be done on pins in a grand piano. Note the 1-1/2 in. section of laminated pin block placed between the jack and the bottom edge of the grand wrest plank to help prevent splitting the wrest plank when driving the tuning pins. This pin block section is moved so as always to be under the area of the piano wrest plank on which the technician is working. Parts: 1) jack; 2) jack plank, 1-1/2-in. section of laminated pin block 3) bottom surface of piano wrest plank; 4) key bed of grand piano.

outer end of the tuning lever. You can easily measure this with a torque wrench. However, it can be measured just as well by tying a string from the end of the tuning lever to a small fisherman's scale (which is inexpensive). If the pressure needed to move the tuning pins falls below 10 pounds at the end of the string or lever, the pins should be made tighter. Usually, to tighten pins without replacing the complete pin block, there are three possibilities:

   1. On an upright, you can take a small punch and drive the tuning pin farther into the pin block. The space between the string coil and the surface of the block or plate should be no less than the thickness of a nickel. When you hit bottom, you are pounding on the back beam of the piano, and can easily break the pin block loose and ruin the instrument.

2. You can apply pin block restorer, which will take from one to two weeks to set properly. Follow the directions on the bottle, and tune the piano later. Also, there is a quick set restorer which is a little more expensive, but sets in from 30 to 60 minutes. It works, too. And you can tune the piano sooner. Be careful not to spill fluids, as they will damage a piano's keyboard or action.

3. If there are not too many loose pins, you can back off the tuning pin a turn or two, carefully lift the string "eye" from the center of the pin, lift the coil, and remove the pin. Then drive in the next-size-larger pin; or, bush the side of the pin with a small piece of veneer, and drive it back in. Some tuners use brass bushings, and some use sandpaper as a positive bushing. The quickest way is to use veneer.

If you attempt any of these repairs on a grand, you must remove the action. Block up the wrest plank securely, using a small jack with

Tilt truck designed by the author. It is constructed of 1-in.-square steel tubing with welded joints. This truck enables an average-sized man to place the heaviest upright piano on its back without strain, and allows the piano to remain at a 120° tilt if desired for other work. The piano can be reset on its base by one man.

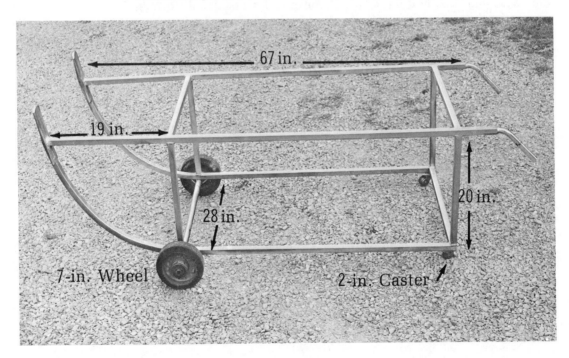

a piece of wood on top of it. Otherwise, you may split the pin block. To remove the grand action, remove the key slip under-screws, which will be found about three-quarters of an inch in from the outer edge of the front of the piano. There will be three to five screws.

Remove the fall board, which will be hinged at each end or fastened to the cheek blocks at either end of the keyboard. The cheek blocks can be removed by taking out the screw which goes through them from the top (often cleverly hidden under a rubber button in the middle of the cheek block), or, it may come up from underneath the key bed into the cheek block. On shifting actions (where the soft pedal moves the action sideways), the keyboard will be held by two small wooden fasteners (one at each end) secured to the key bed with wood screws.

Be certain that *no keys are depressed*. Then carefully slide the complete action toward you and the front of the grand. When it is 8 in. out, stop and look under the pin block to make sure none of the hammers will hit the pin block. If necessary, tilt the action up from the front at this point to clear the pin block with the hammers. Place the action on a smooth, level surface. When you get ready to put it back later, clean out the key bed and sprinkle baby powder on the area where the action rests and slides.

Uprights must be laid on their backs for pin block restorers of any kind to penetrate and do any good. The supply houses sell one-man folding contrivances which will enable you to tilt an upright easily onto its back and up again. You can also have one made. A local welder made a shop truck for the author. It has worked satisfactorily with dozens of pianos in his rebuilding shop.

With the piano on its back, check the casters and sockets. They usually need tightening. This is a good time to tighten the bottom board screws, too. They'll be loose. (That noise you heard when you tilted the piano was caused by hairpins, coins, crayons, etc., falling from under the keys into the strings. Look inside. There are ''fringe benefits'' in this business.)

While you are looking inside, examine the sound board. This one component of the piano makes many sales for an unscrupulous merchandiser. He tells people that a piano with a split sound board is ruined. Perhaps at one time, when modern glues were not available, he had a point. But split sound boards can be repaired. Often the real

Sound board repairs

complaint is a ''buzzing'' which happens when a sound board, whether split or not, has one or more ribs which have come unglued from its back.

To fix sound-board cracks if they are small, one can apply pin block restorer to swell the wood and stop the edges of the crack from vibrating against each other. Of course, if the ribs come unglued, you must drill a small hole from the back to locate the rib center, then drill a larger hole from the front of the sound board through to the rib. Place glue between sound board and rib (modern white glue, Evan's Welch glue, or almost any aliphatic glue will do). Place a wooden washer or sound board button on the wood screw and tighten from the sound board into the rib.

When you find a piano that buzzes, check the sound board and ribs carefully. Also, on uprights, look between the bottom beam and back of the sound board. Chewing gum wrappers, church candles, ping-pong balls, and jacks are often found to be causing the unwanted sounds.

If the sound board is severely cracked, press a mixture of yellow wood filler and aliphatic glue into the crack. If the crack seems too large for stable treatment in this manner, use a sharp chisel to make a wedge-shaped trough along the full length of the crack. Often it helps to drill a small hole at each end of the crack to stop its spreading farther. Make a wedge-shaped piece of spruce the length of the trough (or get a wedge-shaped shim from a supply house), put glue on it, and wedge it securely into the crack. Make the repair level with the sound board front, carefully hand sand it, then varnish or space spray with plastic clear seal.

Bridge repair   Inspect the bridges. When the piano string passes over the bridge, it is angled by two bridge pins. Often in old pianos, and some that are not so old, the pins will work loose because the bridge cap splits slightly. If the split is minor, epoxy filler will fix it. If the split is bad enough to allow the pin to come out with finger pressure alone, the quickest repair is to buy bridge repair plates from a supply house and to follow the simple directions found with them or in the supply catalog. If the complete bridge cap is bad, remove it carefully, following directions in the catalog, and send it to a supplier, where a new cap will be made to fit exactly. Carry some bridge repair agraffes with you. They are inexpensive, and usually install easily.

Sometimes bass bridges work loose. Usually, you will note this at a glance, but whether you observe it or not, suspect it when the bass strings sound dead. To repair such a defect, loosen the bass strings, place wedges between the bass bridge and sound board, fill the space thus created with an application of glue, and remove the wedges. Carefully place the bridge in the position it was when the sound board varnish was new, and drill through the rib into the bridge at each end and at the center. Use wood screws to hold the bridge tightly to the sound board. After the glue has dried, remove the screws, and fill the holes with wooden dowels.

Side and down bearing

To increase the side bearing on a string, get the bridge pins where they belong, or use a bridge repair agraffe. To increase the down bearing so as to give vibrant tone in older pianos, some technicians say you should shim behind the bridge. This is difficult; it is better to simply lift the strings, place thin veneer on the top cap of the bridge (notching the veneer so that it follows the contour of the top cap of the bridge), and thus add to the height of the bridge.

Sometimes a dull tone in the bass will not be improved by these methods. Bass strings are wrapped strings. The wrappings often loosen in older pianos. To repair this, reduce tension on a string so that the end can be removed from the hitch pin. Remove the loop from the hitch pin, turn the string one and one-half to two times *in the direction of the copper winding,* and replace it on the hitch pin. This really makes an improvement in an old "klunker"!

To check down bearing, use a bearing gauge. (Make one by using the dimensions given in the diagram on page 38.) Place the gauge with its center foot resting on the string at its highest point in the bridge. Rock the gauge so that the two outside feet touch the same string in the segments toward the hitch pin and toward the speaking length. The "rock" should be about the thickness of a dime in the treble, and the thickness of a nickel in the bass. Some modern pianos use almost no bearing on the bridge.

A word to the beginning technician: Almost all pianos are made in the same manner, and learning about common troubles and repairs pays off quickly and handsomely. However, both beginners and veterans alike are cautioned that when they're in doubt, check again. In bridge repairs, as in all piano technology, let your motto be, "Do no damage!"

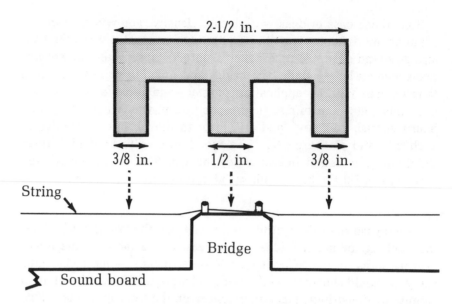

A down bearing gauge can be made from 1/4-in. aluminum stock or harder metal. To use it, place the center foot of the gauge on a string where the string crosses the bridge. Rock the gauge so that the side legs of the gauge touch the running length of the string on either side of the bridge. There should be "rock," as the string should be lower on either side of the bridge than it is on the bridge.

Ten minutes spent in careful measuring and gauging will often save you three hours of hard work. There usually is an easier and more practical way to fix anything. Remember how the piano works in making sound and how the tension of the string is controlled, and most of all, think about what you are doing.

Mastering basic concepts   This first lesson is intended to give an overall view of the basic structure of the sounding section of a piano. No student can properly understand the more advanced considerations of tone production without mastering the concept upon which this foundation of sounding board, transmitting bridges, and string tension is based. The veteran piano technician sometimes finds a review of such things useful as well as practical in locating troubles which at first seem mysterious. Fine tuning depends upon constant consideration of what is happening to this foundation while you tune.

The "first aid" measures set forth in this lesson are precisely that. It is not intended that these measures be used on all pianos, regardless of age or condition, but they will prove useful for making acceptable and even salable pianos out of those which might seem worthless. Dealers who must accept trade-in pianos will find that some of these rapid and economical methods will make a good practice piano out of one that has seemingly passed its prime. And in some cases, technicians will find that a great deal of the dread with which they face the older piano will evaporate.

There are more advanced and complete rebuilding methods given throughout this book. But one need not apologize for using the method that fits the price range and age range of the instrument. In all cases, the objectives are to do a good job and to make a profit. The old piano shall always be with us, and proper techniques can make its strings sing again.

Lesson 2 Tools and supplies for the job

Among my friends is a doctor who carries his medical instruments in a fishing tackle box. His competence as a doctor is not to be questioned, but his choice of an instrument case perhaps creates apprehension among new patients. When taking care of the piano at his home, I am captivated by his five-year-old daughter. Part of her charm is that she loves to put her chubby fingers to work making music. She also compliments me on my "nice doctor's kit"!

You will not hear complaints about your service kit when you are tuning or repairing pianos. Yet, it pays to look professional; your tool case creates a first impression of competence, or lack of it, in the minds of some clients. Eventually, you will think of yourself as a professional piano craftsman, if you do not see yourself as one already. So, it would be wise to buy a good, leather carrying kit as soon as possible. I find it helps my own morale. The supply houses listed at the end of this lesson carry leather service cases.

There seems to be no end to the introduction of new piano technicians' tools. Every so often, a new gadget comes along which does all that is claimed; however, the workman still guides the tool. The basic tools needed and used in this field should be in the kit of every craftsman. Novelties can be added as finances and fancies permit. It has been my experience that it is always better to buy tools which are either chrome plated or made of stainless steel. Although they work the same as other tools, they look better longer.

Also, it is a good idea to purchase or to have someone make a plastic or leather tool roll with compartments for tools. First of all, the rolls keep your tools organized. It is embarrassing to soil your fingers searching through a case full of clanking tools to find just the one you need while your free hand is holding a string loop or perhaps preventing a piano lid from falling. Furthermore, you are working, usually, for a client. Fumbling and disorganization discredits both you and your profession.

Tuning hammer   Your first basic tool is the tuning hammer (so called), which is in reality a tuning lever. Tuning levers come in all sizes, and different sized tips are available to screw on to the handles. Although many technicians state that assuming certain positions while tuning certain pianos necessitates a particular type of hammer head, it is my observation of many years' standing that the shortest head is the best. First, with a short head (certainly no longer than 2 in. in length) you get a better "feel" of the tuning as you proceed. Second, the leverage applied with a short head is less likely to bend the pins. Third, a change of position is better than anything which might increase the distance of the tuner's fingers from the feel of the pin and string while tuning.

Tuning hammers come in different styles. Some are goosenecked. Avoid them. The goosenecked hammer has too much "spring" for a consistent, solid feel of the pin while tuning. Other hammers are extendable. The neck slides down into the handle. This is fine as long as you keep it there! The extra weight of the steel neck reposing in the handle lends authority and power to the tuner. But, once you extend the neck more than an inch or two outside the handle, you lose the vibratory "feel" you want in your fingers as you manipulate the hammer. Besides, you did not make a service call to wrench or bend the pins. You came to tune the piano!

Fine tuning is next to impossible with a long, extended hammer. To those who insist they can tune well with such a hammer, I state unequivocally that their technique must be better than mine and that of all the craftsmen-tuners of my acquaintance. As far as appearances are concerned, fortunately, the supply houses want us to look professional, and almost any tuning hammer you put in your kit will be a real beauty, usually finely turned and handsomely chromed. Get two short heads for your hammer; one a little shorter than the other.

Regulating tools are a must. Again, the supply houses make kits of chrome-plated tools, and offer a complete set of regulating tools which fit interchangeably into a common handle. These come in a rolled container and are your best first buy. Some technicians, however, want a handle on each tool.

Here is a general description of a suitable tuning kit: Ideally, the tools are arranged in one separate roll so that while you are tuning you do not have to search for tools once the tuning kit is opened. Be sure to have a piece of chamois leather or fine felt about 1 ft. wide and 2 ft. long. This material is convenient to spread out on the music shelf once the face of the piano is open for tuning. The cloth serves the special purpose of preventing your tools from making surface marks on the piano. In addition, it will keep you cleaner.

Basic tuning kit

Four rubber mutes are needed: one 6 in. long by 5/8 in. wide, one 3 in. long by 7/8 in. wide, one 3 in. long by 5/8 in. wide, and one 2 in. long by about 1/2 in. wide, and not wider than 1/4 in. at its top. These tapering mutes are used for the following reasons: The first one is placed at the last string going down in the treble, just where the bass strings begin to overlap, in order to quiet the last treble string (which cannot easily be muted with a muting felt strip). The second wide mute is ideally suited for muting the bass strings as one brings unisons to pitch. The last two are used while moving up through the treble after removal of the felt strip, for individual string muting while tuning unisons.

In addition to the above, it is convenient to have a split-rubber treble mute for muting close set strings too short for two mutes, and a felt or leather-tipped treble mute stick, which fits into places other mutes will not.

One or two tapered felt strips, at least 50 in. long, are needed for complete muting for temperament setting, as well as for strip muting of an entire piano when necessary. The Papp treble mute, made of nylon, and featuring an expanding action which takes place automatically, is an asset in tuning. Not only can it be inserted between hammer stems adjacent to the note you are tuning, but it also works efficiently as an action tool to hold the jack and jack spring depressed while you remove or insert butt felts and hammer butt flange screws.

In addition to these tools for tuning, you should have a set of key-easing pliers in your basic tuning kit. Quite often the humidity will

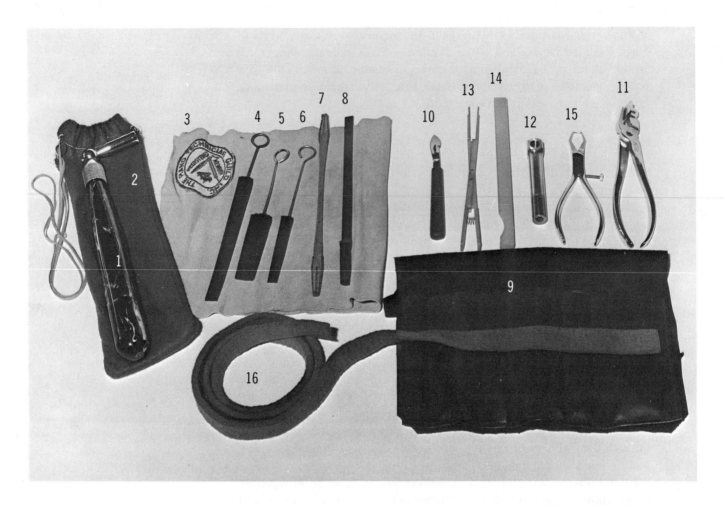

A basic tuning kit: 1) tuning hammer, extendible, with short head; 2) hammer pouch; 3) light-colored chamois field cloth; 4) long mute for bass end of treble section; 5) wide mute for bass strings; 6) short mute for tenor unisons; 7) wood leather-tipped stick mute for treble; 8) split mute with steel handle for treble; 9) tool roll; 10) trimming knife for felt and shank work; 11) key-easing pliers; 12) alternate longer head for hammer; 13) Papp treble mute, with tips slimmed for clearance; 14) mute case; 15) voicing pliers; 16) 52-in. muting strip of soft felt.

cause keys to become sluggish; it is your job to make sure that all keys play on the piano. These pliers, which are equipped with a broad face which swivels on one jaw, will compress the front pin felts in piano keys. Used carefully, these pliers will also satisfactorily compress the upper balance rail bushing on a sticky key.

Voicing pliers, if desired, may be included in the tuning section, although the single needle tool should be used before any drastic hammer voicing is attempted. Voicing hammers, which is explained in a later lesson, is an art, and one which requires great skill. More piano hammers are ruined by crude attempts at voicing than by anything else. Yet, done properly, hammer voicing brings out the uniformity and true beauty of tone of a piano.

Of course, you should have tuning forks in the four most-used frequencies. These are: A-440 cycles per second, which is concert pitch, and today's standard; C-523.3, which is concert pitch; C-517.3, old international pitch; and A-442, a pitch which is being used by several symphony orchestras today, and by concert artists.

Another section of your kit should contain the following regulating and action handling tools:

Regulating kit

One screw-holding device (either an auto mechanic's unit, or one with flexible jaws at the end of a shaft not less than 9 in. long.

A screwdriver handle with a selection of blades, including a Phillips head. Incidentally, it is advisable to always use round-shafted screwdriver blades. The ones with square shafts tend to strike other parts of piano actions and damage or bend them.

Back check wire-bending tool (if possible, one which will also fit other applications, such as bridle strap wires and various linkages within the piano).

Front pin adjusting or turning tool.

Long pair of tweezers.

One double-ended capstan turning tool, with a point on one end and a gradual V on the other for square capstans.

One small hammer head, to fit a universal handle.

One let-off button screwdriver or blade (which is also useful in string repairs).

One pair of good scissors, preferably angled, so that you can see what you are cutting.

One pair of regular pliers.

One bearing gauge.

One curved small file.

One flat mechanic's ignition point file.

One pair of parallel long-nosed pliers for back-check work (and also useful for repairs involving loose jack flanges in wippens when they need to be reglued. This tool is used more often than any other, with the exception of surgeon's locking pliers.)

Locking curved-nose pliers, which are sold in electronic supply stores, by some piano supply houses, and sometimes in surplus stores. These will be used for 60% of your action work, once you get into the habit of using them in place of fingers. Not only will they serve where fingertips cannot go without pushing and breaking adjoining small action parts, but they also lock securely in any one of four positions. They can serve as a small pin vise, a "third hand" while you are trying to complete some operation, and also as an easily inserted bridle tape fastener tool.

Try to keep in mind the picture of a professional. A professional, in any mechanical and technical field, uses tools, not his fingers. Furthermore, piano actions tend to accumulate dust because they are not open for dusting; besides, the small areas involved within their working assemblies would not permit dusting anyway without possible damage to the parts. Good tools well used and used always will keep the piano action in better condition, and the piano technician more professional and clean.

It is helpful if a technician's case contains a large syringe, with a long needle, for application of fluids to various parts and places within the piano. Not only is it possible to accurately measure the amount of flange easing liquid applied in this way, it is also simpler to place fluid drops exactly where you know they will do the most good. Large veterinarian syringes, with 4- or 5-in. needles, can be purchased in some country drug stores, or at farm feed stores and grain elevators. Or, ask a local veterinarian. The syringe is best, but a small-ear, rubber, bulb-type applicator will do the work, although less handily.

String, wire, and pedal repair tools

Other necessities for the individual tool kit are:

A string repair section consisting of one stringing coil lifter for proper alignment of some present coils on the tuning pins to make a more solid tuning.

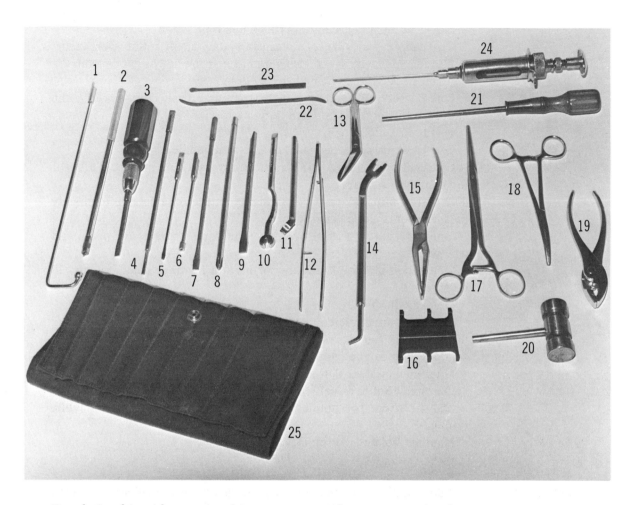

Regulating kit with associated instruments: 1) damper spoon bender; 2) screw holder for flange screws; 3) tool handle which fits all tools, with short screwdriver blade; 4) long blade for damper screws; 5) short, slimmer blade; 6) grand regulation screwdriver with slotted head; 7) long, flat blade; 8) Phillips blade; 9) heavy case screw blade; 10) front rail pin and key spacer adjuster; 11) back check and bridle wire adjuster; 12) tweezers; 13) scissors for felts; 14) capstan regulating tool; 15) parallel pliers for back checks and flanges; 16) bearing gauge; 17) surgeon's locking straight pliers; 18) surgeon's locking curved-nose pliers; 19) pliers; 20) hammer head for tool handle; 21) let-off regulator with slotted end; 22) curved shaping file; 23) flat mechanic's ignition point file; 24) chrome veterinary syringe with 5-in. needle; 25) tool roll.

A pair of music wire cutters (the small type will do).

One caliper type rule for measuring many small action clearances. With toe expanded, it will also serve as a string height gauge from the hammer head center when checking grands.

One center rail bushing punch, for compressing bushings in the center and front of keys when they are too loose.

One tuning pin punch.

One hammer shank reducer (to fit a tool handle).

One center pin punch, which can easily be a fine-pointed scriber if the diameter is small.

One steel 6-in. rule, with equivalents on the reverse side for handy measurements and calculations.

One 7/16 in. by 1/2-in. boxed-to-open-end wrench, for pedal and trap work.

One spool of No. 40 thread, for certain hammer shank repairs in emergencies.

One key dip block.

One piece of fine steel sandpaper (which is intended to be placed in a handle but is sold in hardware stores as "nonwearing" sandpaper; it can be formed to fit desired hammer contours).

One small container of aliphatic glue.

One small bottle of contact cement.

One lid prop, for holding up lids of spinets and uprights while tuning.

Hammer voicing rest block (wood).

Additional tools

Additional tools which you may find useful are: a substitute tuning hammer head, oblong for some old pianos, and with a small recessed tip for European pianos which have small tuning pins; and single and double voicing needles. The author for many years has carried, in addition to these tools, a hollowed handle multitool which contains a chisel, awl, saw, punch, file, reamers, and punches, all in one handle not over 7 in. long. A dentist's slanted mirror is convenient for hard-to-see spots and saves many an action removal. All these tools, fitted in tool rolls, fit into a leather case not over 14 in. long, 6 in. wide, and 7 in. high.

Insofar as supplies are concerned, you will be adding to your inventory as new jobs present new requirements. However, the starting inventory should include:

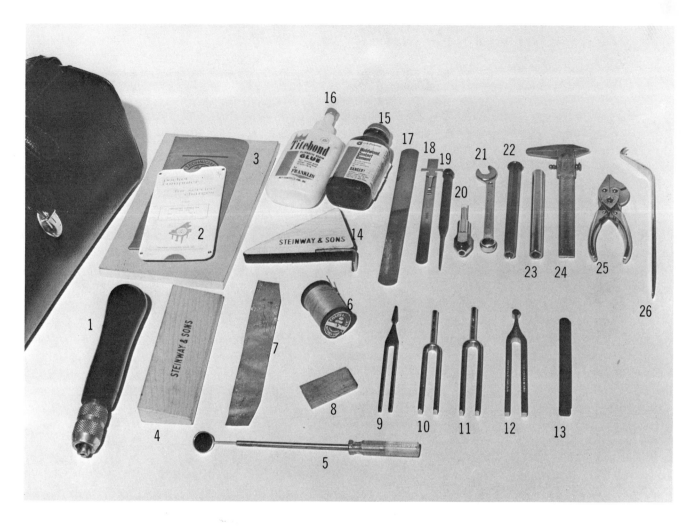

Wire repair, string, and pedal kit: 1) multitool handle; 2) pocket rate computer; 3) billing book; 4) hammer voicing rest block; 5) dental mirror; 6) spool of heavy thread; 7) fine steel sandpaper; 8) key dip block; 9) A-442 fork; 10) A-440 fork; 11) C-517.3 fork; 12) C-523.3 fork; 13) key bushing expander punch; 14) lid prop; 15) contact cement; 16) aliphatic glue; 17) fine ivorine file; 18) 6-in. rule; 19) center pin punch; 20) hammer shank reducer; 21) box-to-open-end wrench; 22) tuning pin punch; 23) coil punch; 24) calipers; 25) music wire cutters; 26) stringing coil lifter and spacer.

Tool case and remainder of tool kit: 1) leather tool kit; 2) multiple-purpose self-contained tool, with assortment of attachments for boring, reaming, filing, and sawing; 3) special oblong head for inserting in tuning hammer, for use on old square grands; 4) voicing needle tool, with two 1/4-in. needles; 5) single needle for voicing, mounted in damper block; 6) hammer voicing rest block; 7) pocket rate computer; 8) billing book; 9) piano action handbook for special measurements in regulating; 10) lid prop; 11) dental mirror.

Catalogs from suppliers
Kit of music wire, sizes 13 to 21, 1/4- or 1-pound rolls
200 balance rail punchings — fine
200 balance rail punchings — medium
200 front rail punchings — light
200 front rail punchings — medium
Assortment of balance rail paper punchings
Assortment of front rail paper punchings
Repair clips for brass rail flanges
Assortment of hammer butt felts
One dozen hammer shanks, 7/32 in.
One dozen hammer shanks, spinet size
One dozen hammer repair springs
Flanges, assorted sizes
Five sets of bridle tapes, cork tipped
300 split strap bridle tapes (for emergency repairs)
One music wire gauge or micrometer
One center pin assortment
Large strip of bushing cloth
One roll of self-adhesive name board felt (used in many ways)

Most of this material is relatively inexpensive. When you order the second time, double your order. Then your stock will always be adequate. Don't buy the cheapest; get the best. Your work is supposed to last in an instrument which may be used for generations. This is only a beginning inventory; established men will have dozens of times this much material on hand and neatly labeled.

Supply houses

American Piano Supply Co.
Box 1005, Clifton, N.J., 07014

Ford Piano Supply
166 East 82nd St., New York, N.Y., 10028

Pacific Piano Supply Co.
11323 Vanowen St., North Hollywood, Calif., 91609

Ronsen Piano Hammer Co.
23 Alabama Ave., Island Park, Long Island, N.Y., 11558

Schaff Piano Supply Co.
2009 N. Clybourn Ave., Chicago, Ill., 60614

Standard Pneumatic Action Co.
855 E. 141st St., New York, N.Y., 10037

Otto R. Trefz, Jr., and Co.
1305 N. 27th St., Philadelphia, Pa., 19121

Tuners Supply Company
94 Wheatland St., Sommerville, Mass., 02145
1274 Folsom St., San Francisco, Calif., 94103
761 Piedmont Ave., Atlanta, Ga., 30308

Classified telephone directories may also list suppliers under "Pianos: Supplies and Parts."

Additional technical information is available from the *Piano Technician's Journal*, P.O. Box 1813, Seattle, Wash:, 98111. Subscribers receive instruction from masters in the field, and questions are answered promptly and clearly.

Lesson 3 Actions found in pianos

Actions in pianos are basically either upright or grand. The differences between upright and grand actions come about mainly because the grand action must be underneath the strings, with the hammers striking upwards, and the basic action on a plane parallel to the position of the hammers while they are at rest. The upright actions are placed in the piano in an upright position, with the hammers perpendicular (or nearly so) to the key bed of the piano. Illustrations of the basic upright and grand actions appear in this lesson.

To identify the various types of actions found in uprights, one needs only to consider the manner in which the linkage is designed, with its main purpose being to connect the capstan end of the key to the wippen of the action.

In the old-fashioned upright action, the wippens were placed at a level some inches above the end of the keys. To span this distance, pieces of wood were usually used, with one end placed at rest upon the capstan of the key, and the other end activating the wippen. Usually, they were tied to the action proper by flange hinge arrangements which kept them up to proper alignment with the action and keys. In some of the older models, the stringer pieces of wood (called *stickers*) were dispensed with, and the capstan screw was elongated a number of inches by means of a wooden adjustable head screwed onto the top, directly under the wippen.

In more recent upright pianos, the height of the piano has been reduced from that of former times, and the length of the stickers has been scaled down accordingly. These larger consoles and studio models usually have no linkage between the capstans and wippen, since their lower height makes it possible to place the upper surface of the key bed reasonably close to the wippens.

Some upright actions are "compressed." This means that the component parts have been shortened wherever possible, so as to place a "direct action" (one in which the key capstan works directly under the wippen) in a piano with an overall height of from 38 to 44 in. In the Wood and Brooks action (now discontinued in manufacture), the action itself is modified to present a low profile when viewed from the side, and to fit into small pianos without having to drop the action below the key bed level. An illustration of the Wood and Brooks action appears on page 58.

Obviously, if a manufacturer wants to keep the action above the level of the key bed, and yet fit it into furniture styled pianos which are quite low in height, he is limited as to how low he may place the key bed, considering that the pianist must sit in front of the piano. Therefore, compressing of the action is one answer.

Drop action In many recent pianos, another way of fitting actions into small pianos has been found. This method is to drop the action below the level of the key bed. How far below depends upon the design department of the piano manufacturer, working with action makers. Generally, the method has worked out as follows: The action is lowered until the hammer rail is at a height approximately the same as the capstan end of the key. To "tie in" the capstan end of the key with the wippen of the action, the same basic "sticker" method is used as in the old upright. But the direction of sticker location is *reversed*. No longer does the sticker rise above the key to travel upward to touch the wippen.

Since the wippen is now many inches *below* the capstan end of the key, the sticker is inverted, and hooked to the forward end of the wippen. Then, when the key is depressed, the end of the key rises, and with it, the end of the action wippen. Basically, all these actions work in the same way, whether they be old-fashioned upright, modern console, or inverted drop action. Regulation and repair of all upright actions proceed along similar lines, with few variations.

Let us suppose that the technician desires to remove an action from the old upright model. He must, as in all pianos, remove the wooden lid or prop it back so as to have a clear field of work. He then removes the upper face panel of the piano. This is usually done by turning small wedges which hold it to the sides, or by removing a few small screws which support it, or by lifting the top retaining catches which secure it to the sides of the case. In the older pianos, the end blocks which hold the face of the piano are removed by taking out screws.

In newer models, end blocks are either nonexistent or come out as a unit with the face panel. In the old upright, the music shelf is secured to the piano with screws, which are usually concealed under the side blocks just discussed. Thus, remove the music shelf.

The action will now be seen, supported by four or more large pedestal screws which come up from the key bed. In addition, it will be fastened in position by three to five knurled knobs, or their substitutes, at the upper end. These hold the action in presentation position before the strings. To the rear of the action, usually on the left side as you face it, there is the damper sustain rod, which comes up from the bottom trap work of the piano, and has its end capped with some quieting substance. It will be aligned with the damper lifter lever which juts back from this end of the action.

At the same end of the action, directly under or slightly to the side of the hammer rail, will be found the soft pedal level rod, which will be secured to the hammer rail, or else will have a doweled end which penetrates into the hammer rail for the purpose of moving the rail when the left-hand pedal is pushed. The nuts must be removed from the action bolts at the upper edge of the action. The damper rod and soft pedal rod must be separated from their connection to the action.

Taking hold of the action brackets and tipping the action about 15° or 20° out from the top will usually allow clearance enough so that the dampers will be free from the strings, and the action brackets will be clear of the action bolts. Then the action is lifted upward and toward the technician. Actions will support themselves on a flat level surface, but will usually be damaged if leaned against anything, in any direction. Don't let the dampers touch anything.

The procedure followed for the old upright model is the same for modern consoles and studio models which have actions completely at a level above the key bed. There will be many times when it is necessary to remove these actions, therefore one should practice until he feels it is mastered. Otherwise, damages done on an outside job when one is unfamiliar with action removal will make hours of extra work, often in places where lighting is less than good. If a technician sustains a loss while removing or replacing the action, the chances are he has damaged the dampers.

To replace standard actions reverse the procedures just described. In all cases, watch the dampers, and avoid changing their alignment.

Removal of the drop action

The instructions which follow are for the Howard spinet piano (see the diagram on pages 78 and 79). While these instructions cannot be followed to the letter on *all* spinet drop action pianos, they are in substance comprehensive enough to enable a technician to remove the action from 80% of all spinets on the market today.

Disconnect the pedal dowels from the action. Disengage pickup fingers from the keys. Remove the four screws (374 in the diagram) which secure the action brackets to the plate. Loosen two action support bolts (379). Remove the screws securing the action rail at each end. The action is now free of the plate, but rests on the two action support bolts threaded into the plate. Note: Tie the thread through the hole (380) and thread the string through corresponding holes in the center brackets; tie onto the opposite end bracket, pulling tight to hold pickup fingers to the action.

The action can now be removed by gripping tightly both center brackets, tilting the top of the action toward you to free the dampers, and slowly and carefully raising the action upwards.

Removal of the Baldwin Acrosonic action

The actions of the 36-in. and 40-in. Baldwin Acrosonic have parts which are standard in size and interchangeable, except for the pickup fingers. (See the diagram on pages 76 and 77.)

To remove these actions: Unscrew the four action bracket bolt knobs (171). Remove the lower frame of the piano and disconnect the pedal dowels from the action. Raise the pickup finger of a note (144) in each of the two end sections of the action as far upward as possible. Tie the heads (159) of these two raised pickup fingers up against the guide rail (162).

Remove the four guide rail screws (162a) attaching the guide rail to the support brackets (161). Push the guide rail back and down against the hammer rail (165) until the hammers touch the strings. Tie the guide rail firmly to the two central action brackets (115). Release the action brackets from the bracket bolts (172) by pulling forward. Note: If the action is equipped with formed steel action brackets (instead of cast iron) the action support rail should be removed with the action. The action can now be removed. Grip both center action brackets tightly. Be careful not to damage dampers.

To replace the Acrosonic action

Reverse the above directions when replacing the action, but be sure the four action brackets rest on the support rail ball bolts. Push the tops of the action brackets onto the bracket bolts, being sure that the brackets are back against the shoulders of the bolts, and taking care to realign the dampers with the strings. Untie the guide rail. Replace and tighten the bracket bolt knobs.

Place a long bar, such as the key strip, immediately in front of the capstan screws (158) and with it, press down the rear ends of all the keys simultaneously. This will permit the pickup finger heads to move readily onto the capstan screws. Bring the guide rail forward, onto the shoulders of the guide rail support brackets. Untie the two raised pickup fingers from the guide rail. Reconnect the pedal dowels to the action. Replace the lower frame.

These instructions are included at this point because the Acrosonic differs somewhat from most drop actions, in that it is a direct blow type action, and removal procedures for other spinets are not adequate for dealing with the Acrosonic.

How the upright action operates

Carefully examine the diagram of a typical upright or drop action presented on the next page. Before we can intelligently begin to regulate actions, we must have a clear understanding of the sequence of operations which takes place in an upright action. The first thing to get firmly fixed in your mind is that *the finger never makes direct contact with the string.*

Although a properly regulated action will seem almost to reflect the exact pulse of the pianist's or tuner's finger, in reality, the action builds up and then releases energy, impacting upon the string, but without a direct chain of contact between the playing end of the key and the string.

When the key is depressed, the downward leverage from the front of the key is transposed into upward motion at the point where the

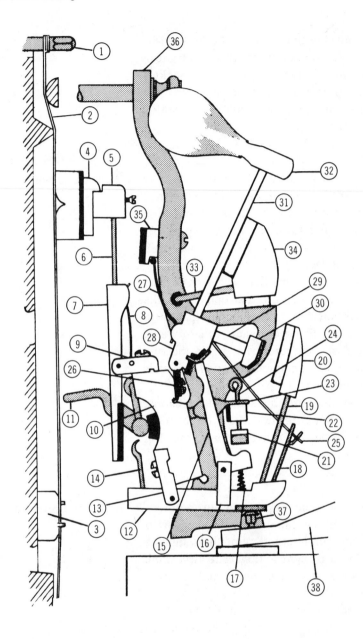

UPRIGHT ACTION

1 tuning pin
2 string
3 bridge
4 damper
5 damper head
6 damper wire
7 damper lever
8 damper spring
9 damper flange
10 action flange rail
11 damper rod
12 wippen
13 wippen flange
14 damper spoon
15 jack
16 jack flange
17 jack spring
18 bridle wire
19 back check wire
20 back check
21 let-off dowels
22 let-off rail
23 let-off rail support
24 regulating screw
25 bridle tape
26 butt flange
27 hammer butt spring
28 hammer butt
29 back stop shank
30 back stop
31 hammer shank
32 hammer head
33 soft pedal level rod
34 hammer rail
35 hammer butt spring rail
36 action bracket
37 capstan screw
38 key

key is pivoted on the center rail balance pin. Attached to the key, and moving upward, the capstan screw, or its related sticker arrangement, causes an upward motion on the wippen, which is pivoting on its flange. At the same instant, the far end of the wippen, pivoting downward, causes the damper spoon to move toward the damper lever.

As the front of the key continues downward, the wippen continues upward, raising the jack, which is pivoting on its flange, and compressing the jack spring. The top of the jack pushes upward on an inclined plane which is the bottom surface of the hammer butt, until such time as the let-off button contacts the forward tail of the jack. At this time, the jack leaves its upward motion and proceeds toward the face of the piano. The back end of the wippen, meanwhile, has advanced during this process to the point where the spoon has contacted the damper lever, which in its further pivot, lifts the felt damper from its position against the strings, preparing the strings to sound.

Immediately upon let off, the hammer, continuing on its propelled path to the string, impacts against the string or unison of strings. The forward motion of the hammer is reversed by its impaction upon the strings, and the hammer moves backward toward the hammer rail. But, with the key still depressed, the back check, which has risen at the same rate as the wippen, is now so positioned that the extended end of the hammer butt contacts the back check surface. This stops the rearward motion of the hammer until the key is released.

At this time, the moment of key release, the hammer returns to its rest position upon the hammer rail and the jack returns to its position under the hammer butt, the wippen returns to its rest position, and the damper lever once again pivots the dampers against the strings.

This is the basic sequence of operations in all upright style actions. It does not vary. Only the necessary clearances required to allow this progression of motions to take place may differ from action maker to action maker. Little else can differ in upright actions. The exact sequence is of great importance. Get it fixed in your mind.

Removing grand actions

Because of the different spatial characteristics of the area where it must be placed, the grand action differs from the upright. And its placement, while precise, is not quite so complicated, especially for removal. Here is how to do it.

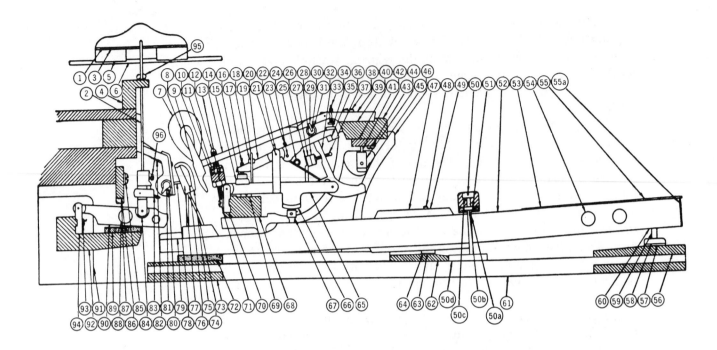

**SECTION OF BALDWIN
GRAND PIANO ACTION**

1 damper head
2 damper wire
3 damper head trim felt
4 damper guide rail
5 damper felt
6 string
7 hammer outer felt
8 hammer under felt
9 hammer molding
10 hammer rail
11 hammer rail cloth
12 hammer rail support prop
13 hammer rail support
     regulating nut
14 hammer shank
15 repetition button felt
16 repetition lever regulating
     button
17 repetition lever regulating
     screw

18 repetition hook felt
19 repetition lever stop hook
20 repetition lever
21 bushing cloth and center pin
22 support flange for repetition
     lever
23 repetition spring regulating
     screw
24 cord for repetition spring
25 repetition spring
26 jack stop spoon
27 jack regulating button felt
28 jack regulating button
29 knuckle insert
30 knuckle under cushion
31 knuckle leather
32 jack
33 drop or repetition screw
34 drop or repetition screw
     cloth

35 jack cushion felt
36 jack regulating screw
37 hammer flange screw
38 hammer flange
39 hammer rail friction covering
40 let-off rail
41 let-off dowel wire
42 hammer flange rail
43 let-off rail screw
44 let-off dowel
45 let-off dowel cloth
46 action bracket
47 key button
48 balance rail pin
49 key button bushing
      (not shown)
50 key strip
50a key strip prop
50b key strip prop fibre nut
50c key strip prop brass nut
50d key strip prop block
51 key strip felt
52 key
53 ivory tail
54 key leads
55 ivory head
55a celluloid front
56 front rail
57 front rail punching (paper)
58 front rail punching (cloth)
59 front rail pin
60 key bushing (not shown)
61 key frame
62 balance rail
63 balance rail punching (cloth)

64 balance rail punching (paper)
65 wippen
66 capstan block cloth
67 capstan screw
68 wippen flange rail
69 wippen rail screw
70 wippen flange
71 wippen flange screw
72 key frame cloth
73 back rail
74 back check wire
75 back check leather
76 back check felt
77 back check head
78 sostenuto pull finger
79 damper lever lifting felt
80 bushing for sostenuto bracket
81 sostenuto rod
82 sostenuto rod bracket
83 sostenuto lever lip
84 damper lever wire flange
85 damper stop rail screw
86 damper stop rail
87 damper lever stop rail felt
88 lead weight for damper lever
89 damper lever board felt
90 damper lever
91 damper lever board support
      block
92 damper lever board
93 damper lever flange screw
94 damper lever flange
95 damper guide rail bushing
96 damper wire screw

Remove the key slip. Take out the fall board; it may be sturdily attached to the key blocks and they may come out with it. Again, refer to Lesson 1. Determine that *no keys are depressed!* Look inside and make sure that no hammers will strike against the piano when the action slides toward you. Look on either side of the action to check if there are small holding blocks there. Remove them if their screws penetrate the key bed. Along the front edge of some actions, which do not slide when the soft pedal is depressed, there will be securing screws. Remove them, and then slide the action carefully toward you. Place it on a flat, level surface.

How the grand action works

Refer to the grand action diagram on pages 60 and 61. As the key is depressed, the same pivotal action takes place at the balance rail as on the upright. The capstan rises, lifting the wippen; the lift of the wippen is transferred to the repetition lever, which starts to lift the hammer knuckle. As the upward motion of the capstan continues, the wippen rises more, and the jack contacts the center part of the hammer knuckle, lifting the hammer toward the string.

Just before the hammer hits the string, the let-off button trips the jack out from under the knuckle. The hammer continues onward to impact with the string, then reverses and heads toward its rest position. By this time, the inside end of the key has made contact with and lifted the damper lever, which has raised the damper from its proper rest position against the string and opened the string for sound. Also, by the time the let-off button has contacted the tail of the jack, the back check, attached to the key itself, has raised to a position where the hammer must contact it if the hammer continues on its way to the rest position (slightly *above* the hammer rail).

Meanwhile, the repetition lever is again in position to support the outer edges of the hammer knuckle, and thus the jack can reposition itself under the knuckle for additional strokes, without the necessity of the key having been released. The "trilling" effect which both concert artist and accomplished pianist find desirable is thus a built-in feature of the grand action.

Related action parts

In the upright, the trap work, which consists of the pedals, their return springs, and levers and dowels, are related parts of the action. This is so because they affect the action, changing its regulation considerably. For example, the right-hand pedal, which operates a long wooden lever that lifts a dowel, pushes up against the damper rod, which is directly between the damper lever bottoms and the action flange rail. The damper levers are kept in proper position with the felt dampers tightly against the strings by the pressure of the damper lever spring which bears against each individual damper. Lifting all the dampers by pressing against the sustain, or right pedal, will reduce the touch pressure needed to depress a key and move the action mechanisms by an ounce or more at the ivory end of the key.

It is clear that such a large change as this in total pressure needed to depress a key will also be a factor in return travel of the key. That is, if the key is binding somewhat, because humidity has swollen the wood, or for other reasons which can easily be encountered, the simple expedient of stepping on the damper sustain pedal will reveal slow travel of the key after it is depressed and released. One of the better ways to check easy key action is to use this information.

Often a key which seems to be returning perfectly well under normal play will show sluggishness. The technician can locate the trouble if he will sustain all the dampers and try the keys for slow return one by one. Also, if there are weak hammer return springs, this method will reveal them, because it removes the extra pressure which the 60 some damper springs have been contributing to the return of the wippen, and thus develops a lesser pull on the part of the bridle strap. With less bridle strap pullback, one can more easily ascertain just how quickly the hammer returns by itself.

Of course, in the lesson on regulation, we will discuss proper setting for the damper actuation, and in the process, eliminate much of the guesswork about action troubles which result when damper springs are offering resistance from the onset of key depression.

Consider the effects of pressing on the left pedal, which in most upright pianos is the ''soft'' pedal. The action of this pedal and its associated trap work results in the hammer rail being advanced toward the strings by 3/4 in. to 1 in. Moving the hammer rail this far forward throws all action regulation into far different part movement relationships than when the hammer rail is in its normal position. By shortening the hammer stroke, the tone is softened. About the only adjustment here that is important is to correct any lost motion between the linkages of the trap work and the hammer rail; then make certain that the bridle tapes are so adjusted that full depression of the soft pedal will not disturb the surface level of the keys.

In most modern uprights, the middle pedal, if there is one, is a smaller factor in the soft mechanism. Some pianos allow the middle pedal to sustain only the bass notes, thus offering an echo effect when top notes are played. Others set the middle pedal trap work so that it modifies the distance to the happy medium between full soft and full normal. In some older uprights, and in some imported pianos, the middle pedal is attached to trap work which activates a long upper bar lying above the hammers. To the bar is attached a long strip of thin felt (which, upon depressing the pedal, will come down between the hammers and the strings), or a "rinky tink" arrangement of metal-ended tabs which occupy the same position and provide a "rinky tink" sound when the pedal is depressed.

Related action parts: the grand piano

The right pedal, or sustain, or "loud" pedal as some call it, in the grand is so designed that the trap work which connects to it lifts the damper lever board, which in turn lifts all the damper flanges, until a stop is reached against the damper stop rail. Changes in the dampers do not play so great a role in changing the touch in grands as they do in uprights, because the spring action of the damper return spring which is found in uprights is not a part of the mechanism in grands.

The left pedal, or "unacorda" pedal, is used in the grand to "shift" the complete action so that the hammers strike only two of the strings instead of three, which they strike in the normal position of the grand action. This shifter pedal, with its trap work, must move freely, and the action must not bind in any way while moving. A large steel spring is located in the side of the piano case, which, bearing against the action frame, forces the action back into normal position when the left pedal is released. Usually the amount of travel is limited by an adjustment screw located in the key block.

The middle pedal on grands is usually the "sostenuto" pedal. This is a selective sustain. For example, if three notes are depressed in the keyboard, and then the middle pedal is depressed, the three notes, or any number which have been depressed, will be sustained as long as the middle pedal is depressed. But additional keys depressed after the middle pedal is activated will not be sustained by the middle pedal. The trap work associated with this sostenuto pedal links with a sostenuto lever rod. The rod holds up damper flanges which are activated before the pedal is depressed. Here is an easy test for this system:

Depress the damper pedal to raise all of the dampers; while holding this pedal down, depress the sostenuto pedal and hold it down. Then release the damper pedal, and check to see that the dampers remain lifted away from the strings, held by the sostenuto mechanism. Then gradually release the sostenuto pedal while watching the dampers. When the pedal has been completely released, all of the dampers should have dropped back onto the strings. Next, depress the sostenuto pedal with no keys depressed.

While the sostenuto pedal is being held down, strike each key a hard blow and release the key. No damper should catch on the sostenuto mechanism and remain away from the string after its key is released. The author has never encountered a simpler or more foolproof method for checking sostenuto.

Adjusting trap work consists mainly of turning nuts in uprights, and lubricating pedal hinge points with nothing less viscous than petroleum jelly (although most lubrication should be with flake graphite or soap). In the grand, minor adjustments are made by alterations of travel of the rods which link the rear of the pedals to the associated parts within the piano case. Most squeaks in trap work are caused by steel spring lips pressing against dry wood or against old compacted felt or leather bushings which have no resiliency.

Always check the places where wood rubs wood, and where wood rubs steel. Lubrication is not as satisfactory as felt or new soft leather bushings. Often a piece of heavy name board felt, either self-adhesive, or affixed with glue, solves problems in these areas that no amount of lubrication will.

Study the illustrations carefully until you are sure you understand the way the action moves and delivers energy to the string. The next lesson will be about regulating the various actions, so a little extra time spent here to better understand actions will save a great deal of time in learning and understanding the next set of techniques.

Lesson 4 Testing and regulating actions

The steps in testing and regulating actions will be given in the order in which they must be followed. It is nearly impossible to do a good job of regulating unless it is done in the correct order.

First, lay the key level. This is a process which requires care and patience, but it establishes the correct dip and key travel, which is the first step in regulating the action. If you use the method outlined here, leveling all the keys is not difficult. It is necessary that you have an assortment of balance rail punchings and an assortment of front rail punchings. These are colored, and thus coded as to thickness. They are reasonable in price, and essential.

Remove the key slip. We are now ready to regulate the level and dip of *an upright action.* Check if there is a pronounced depressed area in the keyboard; in other words, a large number of consecutive keys below the level of the keyboard in general. If this is so, examine the balance rail to determine if it has sunk or warped at a particular level. Loosen the locking screws which hold the particular section to the cross members and adjust with screws (if provided) or with light shims made of paper or veneer until the balance rail is as straight across as you can make it. This saves a lot of extra work.

Now check the height of the highest key at each end of the piano. As a general rule, most pianos can be safely set so that the top of the ivory on the key is 2-1/2 in. from the bottom edge of the key frame. Contact in measuring should be confined to the frame. Do not measure from the key bed. Take your 2-1/2-in. measurement about 1/4 in. from the front edge of the key. Once the highest keys have been set so that their height is as directed, remove or add punchings under the balance rail section of the keys until the various thin or thick punchings raise or lower the keys to a height which is equal to the keys which you have set as a guide at each end of the piano. There are various key leveling devices which you can purchase for sliding along the front edge of the key bed to arrive at the perfect height for each key. For general key leveling, they are excellent. Directions as to their use come with the devices.

Somewhat more precise and offering better response to the pianist is the key leveling method which uses a crowned straightedge. This is done as follows: Establish proper height, as before, for the end keys at bass and treble end of the piano. Block these keys in position at this precise height, either by placing small wedges or key dip blocks under them. Now make the top of each ivory exactly horizontal by comparison to the straightedge. This is done by tapping the balance rail pin to the right or left. Don't let keys touch each other. If they do, use sandpaper to assure clearance.

Place a straightedge which has a 1/32-in. crown in the middle section and reaches from one end of the keyboard to the other. Proceed to insert or remove punchings as in the previous method until the keys are level to the straightedge. Now set the end sharps exactly 1/2 in. above the level of the ivories. Using the straightedge, insert or remove punchings at the balance rail until the sharps are level with the straightedge. Space the sharps before leveling.

Adjust touch   If you measure from a point 1/4 in. back from the front of the key, the maximum depth that the key can be depressed should be 3/8 in. To regulate the depth, insert or remove paper or cardboard punchings at the front rail pins. A key dip block, which is made of wood, is available from supply houses to facilitate this regulation. But be sure it and the key tops are perfectly clean and free from all residues.

Now, check the keys for side play. This is adjusted by turning the oval shaped pin at the front rail so as to allow a slight side motion, to compensate for swelling during damp weather, but with clearance small enough to assure straight downward motion when the key is depressed.

If the small felt bushing at the front of the key is worn, it should be replaced. Remove the bushing by touching it with a piece of felt dampened with hot water, or by steaming it to loosen the glue. Cut a duplicate for the bushing from bushing felt, and install with white glue. Use of a key bushing wedge makes this easier, and also simplifies renewing the key bushing at the top of the center rail pin. Also, bushings can be compressed by the use of a bushing tightener punch, which often remedies the looseness in an older piano. Do not enlarge the hole at the bottom surface of the key where it accepts the center rail pin. On an old piano, if the pins are coated or rusty, clean them with fine steel wool. If the hole for the center rail pin is too large, bush it with cloth or install a patented center rail plastic bushing, available from the supply houses.

Once the key leveling job is done, lift all punchings and felts off the pins and reverse them so that the felt is uppermost in contact with the key. To level the keyboard on a grand, use the procedure just outlined *after* following these directions:

If there are buttons at the balance rail, such as in the Baldwin action, turn them up in order that they will not interfere and prevent the key frame from touching the key bed. Clean out the key bed completely. Install the action, with its key blocks, in the piano. Adjust the key blocks. The key block should exert a moderate pressure on the key bed frame pin when it is secured to the key bed. Now tap downward along the front of the key frame to locate any knock. A knock will indicate that the front frame rail does not properly contact the key bed at some point.

Bed the key frame

In Baldwin grands, the key frame has been slightly hollowed from back to front. Thus the front and back touch the key bed, but the center rail is held above the key bed by the key-bed buttons. When the key frame is properly set in the key bed, the contact along the front rail edge should be complete. If a knock is found, mark the places where knocks begin and end, and lightly sand away all places where there is no knock between frame and bed. This is done by using 3/0 sandpaper between the front edge of the key frame and key bed, drawing it in and out, and sanding the key frame. Don't try to shim the frame to get rid of knocks. For other-make grands, slightly different arrangements are sometimes made. But in all cases, the goal is to get the key frame sitting securely on the key bed at the front rail, so as to have definite regulating.

Now, regulate the capstan screws so that the hammer shanks clear the hammer rest rail. Make sure that the action assembly is properly in the piano, then measure the distance from the bed to a point 1/4 in. back on the ivories in extreme treble and bass. Proper height is 2-9/16 in. in Baldwin concert grands, 2-1/2 in. for all other Baldwin and Hamilton grands, and 2-3/8 in. for Howard grands. Exact measurements for key height and key dip, in inches, for pianos of other manufacturers, as compiled by the author, are given in the table on page 71.

Once the proper measurements at each end are made, proceed to set the key level on the grand in the manner used on uprights.

Regulation of the upright action

Level the keys. Regulate the dip. Adjust the capstan screw on the end of the key to lift the jack so that it is just touching the hammer butt, but without lifting the hammer stem away from the rail (especially in extremely damp weather). Under normal humidity conditions, back off the capstan after this adjustment until there is just a "suspicion" of lost motion between hammer butt and jack. Make sure the hammer rail is completely at rest, and the hammers will move 1-7/8 in. from rest position to touch string. If the distance is too long, space the hammer rail properly; if too short, lower the hammer rail. A table of hammer distances for various manufacturers follows this lesson, but as a rule, 1-7/8 in. hammer travel is right.

Gently "travel" the hammer to the string by hand, and make sure that it is striking all three strings at once. If it is off center, loosen the flange, and center the hammer to the strings. If not corrected in this way, heat the hammer shank and bend it slightly in the desired direction.

Adjust the let-off rail buttons so that the buttons center on the jack fly, and trip out the jack from under the hammer butt when the hammer is 1/8 in. from the strings. (This varies by 1/32 in. in some makes of pianos. Of course, when possible, get a service manual and follow its specifications exactly.) The jack must trip out far enough to allow the hammer butt to return without dancing upon the tip of the depressed jack. If the jack trips out too far, it makes noise upon striking the rail.

See that the dampers rest smoothly and squarely on the strings. Adjust the damper spoons, if necessary, so that the dampers just begin to lift when the hammer has traveled halfway to the strings.

	Key height in inches	Key dip in inches	Table of key height and dip
Baldwin			**Grands**
Model D	2-9/16	3/8	
Models M, R, L, F	2-1/2	3/8	
Kimball			
Models B and D	2-3/4	13/32	
Model G	2-3/4	3/8	
Sohmer	2-3/8	3/8	
Steinway	2-5/8	3/8+(.390)	
Wurlitzer	2-5/8	3/8	
Acrosonic	2-1/2	7/16	**Uprights**
Betsy Ross	2-3/8	3/8	
Cable	2-1/2	7/16	
Estey	2-3/8 to 2-5/16	3/8 to 7/16	
Everett	2-1/2	7/16	
Kohler and Campbell	2-3/8	7/16	
Krakauer			
37- and 38-inch models	2-9/16	7/16	
40-inch model	2-1/2	7/16	
45-inch model	2-5/8	7/16	
Kranich and Bach	2-1/2	7/16	
Laughead	2-5/16	7/16	
Mason and Hamlin	2-1/2	13/32	
Sohmer			
Direct Blow	2-7/16	3/8	
Drop Action	2-1/2	13/32	
Starck	2-7/16	7/16	
Steinway	2-3/8	3/8+(.400)	
Story and Clark	2-3/8	7/16	
Console	2-5/16	13/32	
School Model	2-5/8	3/8	
Winter	2-1/2	7/16 (Scales E, K40-3/8)	
Wurlitzer			
37-inch model	2-9/32	13/32	
40-and 44-inch models	2-11/32	3/8	

For finer touch and less damper resistance, set the dampers to lift when the hammer is 5/8 in. from the strings. Reach under the wippens with a spoon bender, catch the damper spoon wire, and bend it in or out.

Set the back checks so that the hammers stop on rebound 5/8 in. from the strings. Some technicians set the first and last back check in each section and space all others in line with them, and on new or nearly new pianos this will work. But on worn action, back checks should not be spaced for beauty, but to stop the rebound 5/8-in. from the strings.

Depress the soft pedal (on the left) and see that the bridle tapes are just taut when the soft pedal is fully depressed. Bridle tapes must not "ripple" motion surfaces of the keys.

Depress the sustain (right) pedal and make sure that the dampers lift upon full depression the same amount as they do upon full depression of the natural key. Adjust pedals accordingly. Dampers should all seat fully when the sustain pedal is within 1/4 in. of being completely released. (Measure this from the front surface of the piano where the pedal comes through.) There should always be a little lost motion between the sustaining rods and the action, so that the dampers rest on the strings and not on the sustain levers. (See diagram, pages 74 and 75.)

Pickup fingers, etc.   As previously mentioned, upright actions in modern pianos are often "dropped," and extending stickers are used to connect the action with the ends of the keys. While some minor problems may develop in regulation if the technician does not obtain proper lift without lost motion in these fingers, ordinarily it is mostly a matter of seeing the stickers as an extension of the capstan and treating them accordingly, then proceeding to regulate the action itself according to upright procedures. To better understand the necessary engineering differences between upright actions and those which have been dropped lower in the piano, the Acrosonic Full Blow and Howard actions are shown on pages 74 through 79.

Regulating the grand action   With the action in the piano, and with all previous operations as to key level and hammer lifted position accomplished, test and regulate the extreme hammers in each section so that they are 1-7/8 in. from the strings by "trueing" them with the turning of capstans. Then remove the action from the piano, and place it upon a smooth and level bench. (See the diagrams on pages 60 and 80.)

Turn the jack regulating screws so that the extreme jacks in each section are set with their back edges in line with the back edge of the small wooden insert in the knuckle. This applies when you encounter knuckles which are perfectly rounded. When the knuckles are partially round, or pear-shaped, set the back edge of the top of the jack 1/16 in. back of the front face of the wood in the knuckle. To see what you are doing in this operation, you must depress the repetition lever slightly. At the same time, support the hammer shank in its correct-height position at the hammer rest rail. Otherwise, you will get an incorrect adjustment, for the hammer will tend to drop, and thus the knuckle will not be where you thought it was.

Once you have the extreme jacks set properly, regulate the remaining jacks. This is done as follows: First, raise all of the hammers of a section. Then place a weight across the rear ends of the keys (just behind the back check wires) to hold them down. Stretch a taut thread between the edges of the already adjusted extreme jacks in each section. Adjust the remaining jacks so that their edges line up with this thread. The thread may be kept taut by attaching a small weight to each end. Repeat for each section.

With the hammers raised, check by a touch of the finger to see that the height of the jack is about 1/64 in. below the top surface of the cradle of the repetition lever. Turn the repetition lever regulating screw up or down to make the necessary adjustment. Return the hammers to rest position.

Set tops of jacks

Place the action in the piano. Raise a hammer toward the strings by slowly depressing a key. The hammer should rise to within 1/16 in. of the string and then "let off" (become mechanically disengaged from the key due to the operation of an escapement mechanism in the action). Adjust the let-off dowels (or regulating buttons in some pianos) to permit the hammers to let off 1/16 in. from the string.

While the action is in the piano, recheck the adjustment of the end hammers in each section to be sure that they are set 1-7/8 in. from the strings. Reset if necessary by turning the capstan screws.

Check hammer let-off and hammer stroke

201 bracket bolt knob
202 bracket bolt
203 damper block set screw
204 damper block
205 damper molding
206 damper felt
207 string
208 damper wire
209 hammer butt spring rail
210 spring rail felt
211 spring rail attach screw
212 hammer butt spring
213 hammer butt
214 hammer butt skin
215 hammer butt cushion felt
216 hammer butt felt
217 damper lever spring
218 damper lever flange attach screw
219 damper spring cord
220 center pins and bushing cloth
221 damper lever flange
222 damper lever
223 hammer flange
224 hammer flange attach screw
225 main action rail
226 damper rod flange

227 damper rod (all dampers)
228 damper rod bumper felt
229 damper lever felt
230 damper lever spoon
231 wippen flange attach screw
232 wippen flange
233 wippen
234 action bracket
235 key cloth
236 ball bolt
237 key frame back rail
238 hammer felt (outer)
239 hammer felt (under)
240 hammer molding
241 hammer shank
242 hammer rail felt
243 hammer rail
244 hammer rail hook
245 hammer rail blocking felt
246 hammer butt heel stem
247 hammer butt heel
248 hammer butt heel bumper felt
249 hammer butt heel skin
250 back check felt
251 back check
253 bridle strap
254 regulating button screw eye

255 regulating rail attach screw
256 regulating rail screw
257 regulating rail
258 regulating button
259 regulating button punching
260 back check wire
261 bridle wire
262 jack
263 jack spring
264 jack flange
265 capstan screw felt
266 capstan screw
267 key button
268 balance pin
269 ivory tail
270 ivory head
270a celluloid front
271 key
272 front rail pin
273 key frame front rail
      punching (cloth)
274 key frame front rail
      punching (paper)
275 key frame front rail
276 key bed
277 key frame cross rail
278 key frame balance rail
      punching
279 key frame balance rail

HAMILTON UPRIGHT ACTION

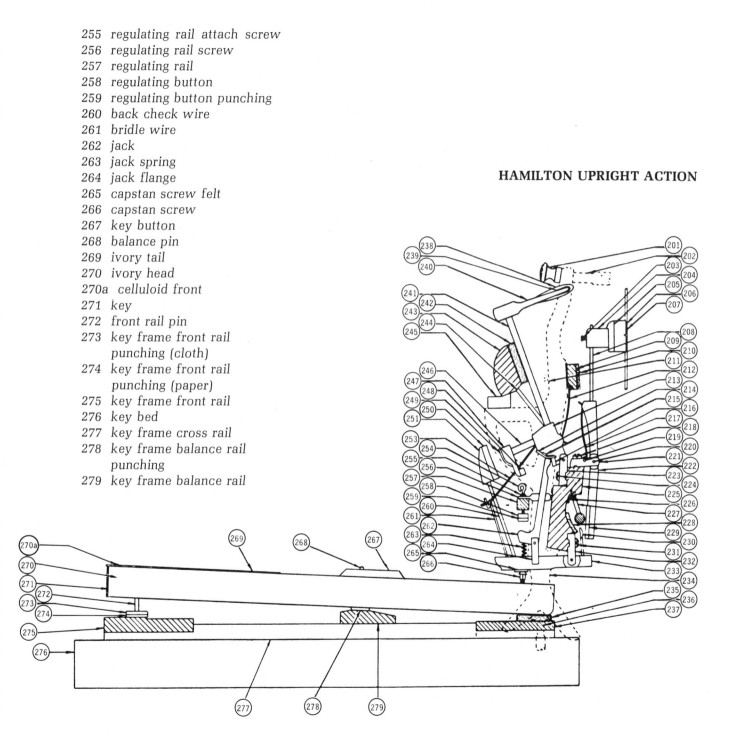

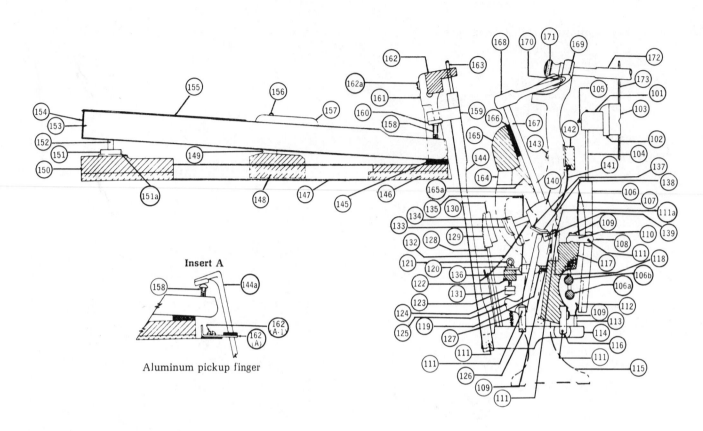

Insert A

Aluminum pickup finger

ACROSONIC
FULL BLOW ACTION

101 damper block
102 damper molding
103 damper felt
104 damper wire
105 damper block set screw
106 damper lever
106a damper rod (all dampers)
106b damper rod (bass dampers)
107 damper lever spring
108 damper lever flange
109 flange attaching screws
110 damper spring cord
111 center pins
111a center pins bushing cloth
112 damper lever felt
113 damper lever spoon
114 wippen

115 action bracket
116 wippen flange
117 main action rail
118 hammer flange
119 regulating rail screw
120 regulating rail attaching
      screw
121 regulating screw eye
122 regulating rail
123 regulating button
124 regulating button punching
125 jack
126 jack flange
127 jack spring
128 back check wire
129 back check
130 back check felt

131 bridle wire
132 bridle strap
133 hammer butt heel skin
134 hammer butt heel
135 hammer butt heel stem
136 jack bumper felt
137 hammer butt skin
138 hammer butt cushion felt
139 hammer butt felt
140 hammer butt
141 hammer butt spring
142 hammer butt spring rail
143 spring rail attaching screw
144 pickup finger
144a aluminum pickup
      finger (see insert A)
145 key cloth
146 key frame back rail
147 key frame cross rail
148 key frame balance rail
149 key frame balance rail
      punching
150 key frame front rail
151 key frame front rail
      punching (cloth)
151a key frame front rail
      punching (paper)
152 front rail pin

153 key
154 key front
155 key covering
156 balance rail pin
157 key button
158 capstan screw
159 pickup finger head
160 pickup finger cloth
161 pickup finger guide rail
      bracket
162 pickup finger guide rail
162a pickup finger guide rail
      screw
162(A) pickup finger guide rail
      (see insert A)
162(A-1) pickup finger guide
      rail screw (see insert A)
163 pickup finger guide pin
164 hammer rail blocking felt
165 hammer rail
165a hammer rail hook
166 hammer rail felt
167 hammer shank
168 hammer molding
169 hammer felt (outer)
170 hammer felt (under)
171 bracket bolt knob
172 bracket bolt

301 damper block
302 treble damper backing and felt assembly
303 treble damper felt
304 damper wire
305 damper block set screw
306 damper lever
306a damper rod (all dampers)
307 damper lever spring
308 damper lever flange
309 flange attaching screw
310 damper spring cord
311 center pins
311a center pin bushing cloth
312 damper lever felt
313 damper lever spoon
314 wippen
315 action bracket
316 wippen flange
317 main action rail
318 hammer flange
319 regulating rail bracket
320 regulating rail attaching screw
321 regulating screw eye
322 regulating rail
323 regulating button
324 regulating button punching
325 jack
326 jack flange
327 jack spring
328 back check wire
329 back check
330 back check felt
331 bridle wire
332 bridle strap
333 catch skin
334 catch
335 catch stem
336 jack bumper felt
337 hammer butt skin
338 hammer butt cushion felt
339 hammer butt felt

340 hammer butt
341 hammer butt spring
342 hammer butt spring rail
343 hammer butt spring rail attaching screw
344 pickup finger
345 key cloth
346 keyboard back rail
347 keyboard cross rail
348 keyboard balance rail
349 keyboard balance rail punching
350 keyboard front rail
351 keyboard front rail punching (cloth)
351a keyboard front rail punching (paper)
352 front rail pin
353 key (natural)
354 key covering
355 key front
356 balance pin
357 key (sharp)
358 locknut
359 pickup finger felt punching
360 key fork
361 grommet
362 pickup finger bushing
363 action strap
364 attaching screw (action strap to support rail)
365 attaching screw (action strap to bracket)
366 lockwasher (action strap to bracket)
367 hammer rail blocking felt
368 hammer rail
368a hammer rail hook
369 hammer rail felt
370 hammer shank
371 hammer molding
372 hammer felt
372a hammer underfelt

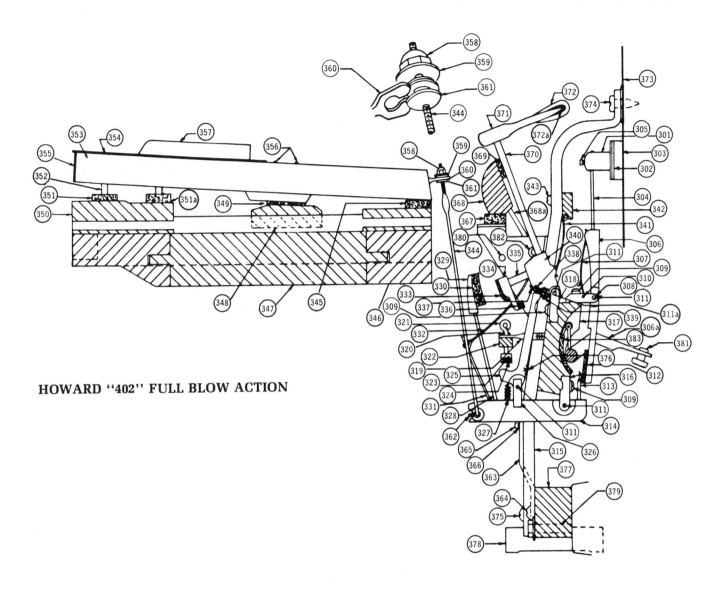

HOWARD "402" FULL BLOW ACTION

373 string
374 attaching screw (action
     bracket to plate)
375 attaching screw (action brack-
     et to action support rail)
376 attaching screw (action
     bracket to action rail)
377 action support rail

378 action support rail support
     block
379 action support bolt
380 string hole (action bracket)
381 grommet (damper rod)
382 grommet (hammer rail
     support)
383 action rail felt

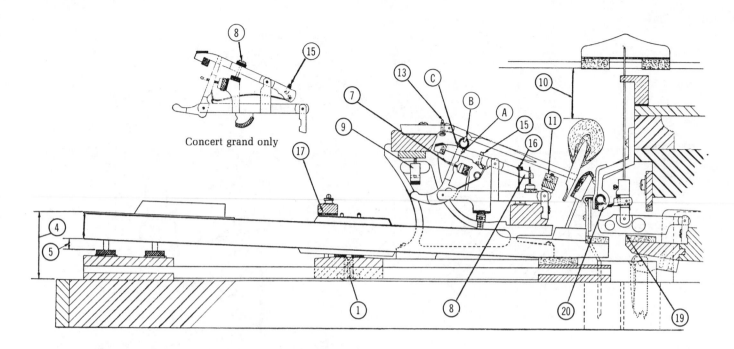

Concert grand only

BALDWIN GRAND REGULATION STANDARDS

1 Set key frame buttons paper thickness above key bed with keys removed.
2 Center hammers under strings.
3 Space repetition levers.
4 Square, level, and space keys. (Be sure that hammer shanks clear hammer rest rail first). Height of keys 1 and 88 to be set as follows: Baldwin Concert Grand, 2-9/16 in; all other Baldwin and Hamilton Grand pianos, 2-1/2 in; Howard Grands (Style 474), 2-3/8 in; all sharps to be 1/2 in. above ivories.
5 Set touch depth 3/8 in. measuring 1/4 in. back from front of natural key.
6 Set end hammers of each section 1-7/8 in. from strings.
7 Set surface "A" of jack in line with surface "B" of knuckle insert by adjusting screw.
8 Regulate repetition lever so that it is 1/64 in. above top of jack at "C".
9 Set "let-off" 1/16 in. from string.
10 Re-check hammer stroke to be 1-7/8 in. on end hammers of each section.
11 Set hammer rest rail 1/8 in. below end hammer shanks.

12 Set hammer line 1-7/8 in. from strings, lining up on end hammer of each section.
13 Set "drop" to 1/16 in.
14 Set back checks to catch hammers 5/8 in. from strings.
15 Regulate repetition spring so that hammer will rise without a jump.
16 To set repetition lever stop hook, press hammer down 1/4 in. below its checking point on back check. The stop hook should then come into contact with the felt. Concert Grands need no adjustment. (Stop hook not present in all actions).
17 Set key strip so that front of a natural key can be raised 1/8 in.
18 Damper should start to lift when hammer is 7/8 in. from strings.
19 Have 1/16-in. clearance between felt on damper lever board and damper levers.
20 Set sostenuto rod lip to clear 1/16 in. between it and damper lever lip, viewed from front; set sostenuto rod bracket so that sosenuto rod lip projects 1/16 in. under sostenuto lever lip with pedal depressed (viewed from above).

Set hammer rest rail   Place the action on the bench. Adjust the hammer rest rail so that it is 1/8 in. below the bottom of the extreme hammer shanks in each section. Adjustment is made by turning the nuts on the hammer rail support props. Be sure to tighten the lock nuts after this adjustment.

Using the end hammers of each section as a guide, adjust the capstan screws of all of the other notes in the section so that the hammers line up with the end hammers (the end hammers having already been set 1-7/8 in. below the strings in the previous step).

Adjust hammer drop   With the action assembly on the bench, raise each hammer slowly to let-off by gradual depression of the key. A very slight further depression of the key should cause the hammer to drop slightly as the jack slips out from under the knuckle. Adjust the hammer drop screw which is located in the hammer shank flange so that the amount of the drop is 1/16 in. A gauge which represents the string height is useful for performing this operation.

Regulate back checks   When the key is struck a medium blow and held down, the hammer, after it rebounds from the string, should be caught and held at a distance of 5/8 in. from the string by the back check. To regulate the back checks, first, with the action on the bench and with a straightedge held against the back of the back check heads, rotate the back check heads on their wires until the backs of the heads are parallel to the straightedge (this should make the back check felt parallel to the hammer heels). Then space each back check to the center (right and left) of the hammer heel as nearly as possible without having the back check touch the adjacent hammer. When spacing, be sure to keep the sides of the back check heads vertical.

Regulate the back checks so that the hammer catches 5/8 in. from the string by tapping the back check heads toward or away from the hammer molding with the finger. To judge when the hammer is checking 5/8 in. below the string with the action on the bench, recall that the hammers have just previously been set so that let off and drop are each 1/16 in. Thus, if a hammer catches 5/8 in. away from the string, it will be positioned about 1/2 in. below an adjacent hammer which has been allowed to let off and drop.

When regulating back checks on the bench, strike the key hard enough to insure that the hammer will catch on the back check, but not hard enough to cause it to swing up beyond a vertical position of the shank; otherwise the hammer shank may strike against the drop screw and damage the wood at its center, or it may bend the center pin. The speed and accuracy of the back check adjustment may be improved by raising three or four hammers at one blow. When properly adjusted, they should check at the same height.

The accuracy of the back check adjustment should be checked by placing the action in the piano to make sure that the hammers are caught about 5/8 in. from the strings. When regulating back checks, take care that the hammer heel does not contact the back check when the hammer is on its way up to the string, as this will prevent full response of the action during loud playing. Hammer clearance may be tested with the action on the bench by depressing each key slowly with one hand while gently restraining the corresponding hammer with the other hand. Be sure the back check does not touch the hammer heel as the hammer rises.

Regulate repetition springs, repetition stop hook, and height of key strip rail

With the action still on the bench, strike the key so the hammer checks (catches). Then release the key slightly; the hammer should rise, without lagging or a pronounced jump. Regulate the spring by turning the repetition spring regulating screw on the repetition lever.

With the action still on the bench, strike the key so that the hammer checks. While holding the hammer in check, press it down 1/4 in. further on the back check. With the hammer in this position, the repetition stop hook should be touching the felt on the lever. Turn the hook up or down, as may be necessary. (Note: Concert grands and some other Baldwin grands do not have a repetition lever stop hook, and require no adjustment.) Be sure the stop hook does not interfere with the repetition lever.

The height of the key strip rail should be regulated so that the front of the naturals can be raised a scant 1/8 in. Adjust by removing the brass lock nuts and turning the fibre nuts underneath the rail. Test by holding down the key strip rail while raising the keys. When adjustment is correct, reinstall and tighten the brass lock nuts.

Dampers

Check the dampers to see that they are seated squarely on the strings and move up and down freely. Test each key to make sure that the damper rises to clear the strings when the key is depressed and that the damper returns and seats properly on the strings when the key is released. If any dampers work sluggishly or stick and do not return to the strings, the bushings in the damper guide rail hole can be reamed gently by means of a semitubular umbrella wire tapered at the end for easy insertion. Do not twist the reamer in the bushing as this will enlarge it too much.

The damper should start to lift when the hammer is 7/8 in. from the string. If necessary, adjust by thinning or building up the damper lever lifting felt. Damper levers, when at rest, should be 1/16 in. above the damper lever board felt. This allows the damper pedal to travel about 1/4 in. before the dampers start to lift. Adjust by adding or removing leather punchings from the damper pedal rod socket at the rear of the pedal. When the damper pedal is used, all dampers should lift evenly and simultaneously. If adjustment is necessary, glue in or remove paper shims under the damper lever board felt. It is highly undesirable to change the adjustment of the damper wire by loosening the damper wire screw, unless it is evident that the original factory adjustment has been disturbed. (Changing this adjustment may make it difficult to secure proper damping action.)

Check the setting of the damper stop rail by making the following test on a few representative keys in each section having dampers: Depress the key fully, and with the other hand gently try to lift the corresponding damper head beyond its normal raised position. There should be no play in the black-key dampers but some slight play in the naturals. If adjustment is required, reset the damper stop rail after first removing the small nails which prevent it from being jarred out of place. Then loosen each damper stop rail screw and adjust the corresponding section of the rail. Tighten the screws and replace the nails when the adjustment has been completed.

Regulate sostenuto   First, regulate the sostenuto lever lips so that they are all in alignment. The in or out adjustment can be made by bending the damper wire right above the damper lever wire flange in or out. The up or down adjustment can be made by inserting a small piece of paper in the sostenuto lever lip just below the bumper cloth. When in proper adjustment, the bottom of the sostenuto rod lip should be 1/16 in. above the bottom edge of the sostenuto lever lip, as viewed from the front. Set the sostenuto rod by bending in or out the brass bracket so the sostenuto rod lip projects back underneath the sostenuto lever lip 1/16 in. when the pedal is depressed. Do not use paper or cardboard shims to block out sostenuto rod brackets.

Let-off gauges and racks are available from supply firms, and, as you can see, are not absolutely necessary if each step in grand regulating is done precisely. While grands of various makers may differ in the quality of their engineering and often lack a service manual to guide the technician, the basic techniques as described should be memorized. Grand actions can be regulated properly only by such techniques; they deserve the care and patience of a competent craftsman. In all cases, learn the methods which are approved by skilled craftsmen and by solid, service-minded piano manufacturers and use them on all your work.

Regulation such as was described may not be fully appreciated by a person who considers the piano a piece of furniture, but the technician himself can take pride in doing a thorough job, and the musicians among his clientele will know the difference.

Special instructions

Often a proper regulating job is almost impossible unless the component parts are up to standard specifications. In every case, where hammers are badly grooved, you must include resurfacing (covered in a special repair lesson) or replacement. Further, as your professional activity expands, keep your clientele informed of the need of proper regulation if the piano is to perform as it should. There is no reason why ignorance of piano technology on the part of a client should keep you from sharing your wealth of information. People should have been informed long ago that the piano has thousands of interacting parts and that *it is the responsibility of the piano craftsman to make certain they are interacting as they should.*

As you can see, the old carpenter's axiom "Measure twice and saw once" holds true when you try any kind of regulating. Measure the proper distances before touching anything or changing it. The better piano manufacturers consider the tolerances given in their service manual to be precisely in accordance with design and engineering for achieving the desired level of performance. Adherence to the specifications will make the piano perform as its maker intended. To use up tolerances indiscreetly, hoping to do a better job than the original designer did, is to misalign the action and to prevent an additional benefit which accrues when the key and action interact as they were designed to do. This benefit is called "after-touch."

After the blow by the piano player has resulted in the proper flow of power through the action, the remainder of the unexpended power and action travel accumulates in, and is absorbed by, the after-touch portion of key travel. No accurate measurement can be given for this elusive phenomenon, but it will be properly dimensioned if all regulating tolerances are accurate to the manufacturer's specifications. Reasonable allowance has been made by the piano maker for continued use, wear, and climatic variations.

There is a ratio of balance between the center rail pin point in the key and the distance to key front, and from center rail balance point to capstan. Moving the capstan screws forward or backward along the key throws out of ratio this highly specialized design. There is what is called an "action spread" in every piano (the straight line measurement between the center pin of the wippen flange and the center pin of the hammer flange). Key ratio and action spread are purposely complementary to each other in a well-designed piano. To alter one is to seriously misalign the other. Tolerances were not provided for use by technicians. They were provided to compensate for wear and humidity changes.

Depth of touch is of great importance in a piano. If a piano has a hammer stroke of 1-7/8 in. and a key dip of 3/8 in., the key movement is in a ratio of 1 to 5 with the hammer movement. When the hammer let-off point is reached, the ratio is changed (considering the amount of key travel still left as the hammer lets off) to about 1 to 7. So what seems to be but a small imperfection in the laying of the touch at the keyboard will result in imperfect follow through. The resultant complaints will be: "I can't get this thing to give out the power I want . . . the repetition is poor . . . something seems to make the sound mushy."

Since world renowned concert pianists, who have devoted a lifetime to the mastery of the piano, fail to recognize the presence of after-touch, it is understandable that piano technicians may also fail to note this important facet of action work. Considering the small amount of the total key travel provided for after-touch, it is necessary to have good control of keys while observing hammer movement. With the key slip removed, place the tip of the finger on the key bed with the key front in contact with the finger. Adjust finger pressure so the key can be moved but yet held at any point of travel.

In this manner, the precise point of let-off and hammer drop can be observed. Movement of the hammer after drop indicates excessive after-touch. In such cases, the action is not regulated according to the original design or the original design has been modified. In cases where the action is properly regulated but there exists inadequate after-touch, the length of the hammer stroke can be reduced or increased a small amount to obtain proper after-touch.

The following diagrams are cross-sections of the Wood and Brooks actions. Early in the twentieth century, Wood and Brooks produced about one hundred thousand actions annually, nearly one-third of all the actions used. Since parts nomenclature is fairly standard, the parts for the first diagram, the grand action, have not been numbered or named. Subsequent diagrams are labeled.

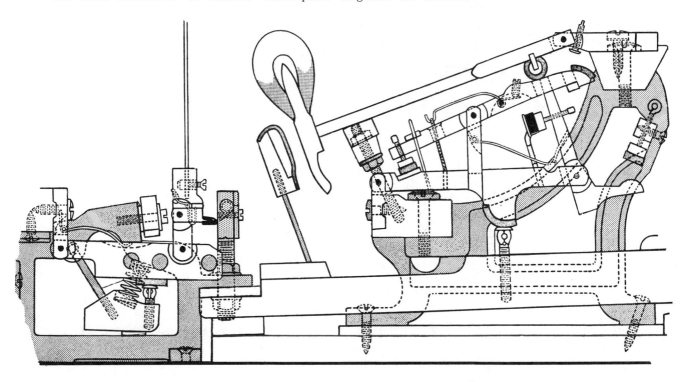

W & B GRAND ACTION

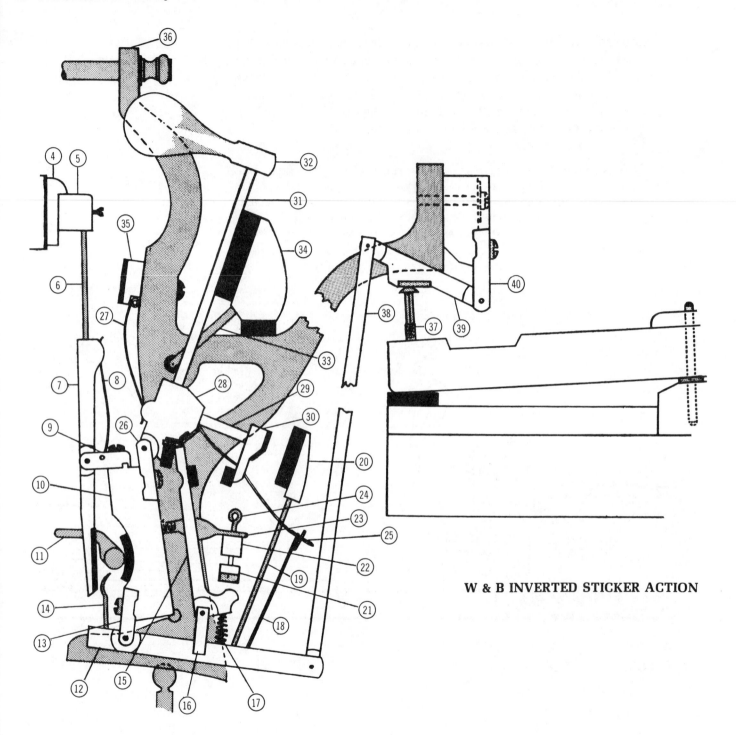

W & B INVERTED STICKER ACTION

This key is for the diagrams on pages 88 and 89.

W & B SUPERIOR CONSOLE DROP ACTION

1-3 not shown
4 damper
5 damper block
6 damper wire stem
7 damper lever
8 damper spring
9 damper flange
10 action rail
11 damper lift arm
12 wippen
13 wippen flange
14 damper spoon
15 jack fly
16 jack flange
17 jack spring
18 bridle tape wire
19 back check stem
20 back check
21 let-off button
22 let-off peg
23 let-off rail
24 let-off screw
25 bridle tape
26 butt flange
27 hammer return spring
28 hammer butt
29 back catch stem
30 back catch
31 hammer shank
32 hammer
33 hammer rail bracket
34 hammer rest rail
35 damper stop felt
36 action bracket
37 sticker adjuster
38 drop sticker
39 drop lifter
40 key flange

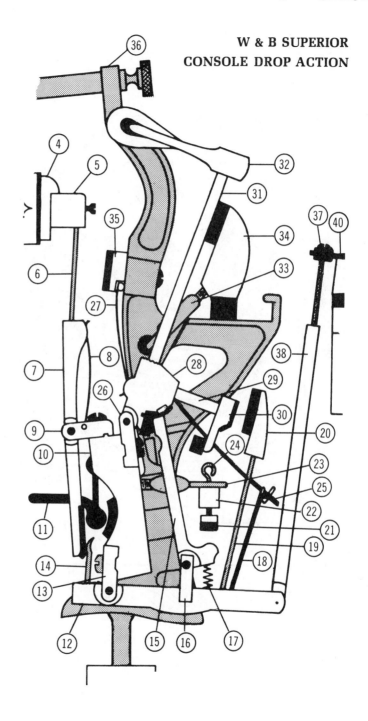

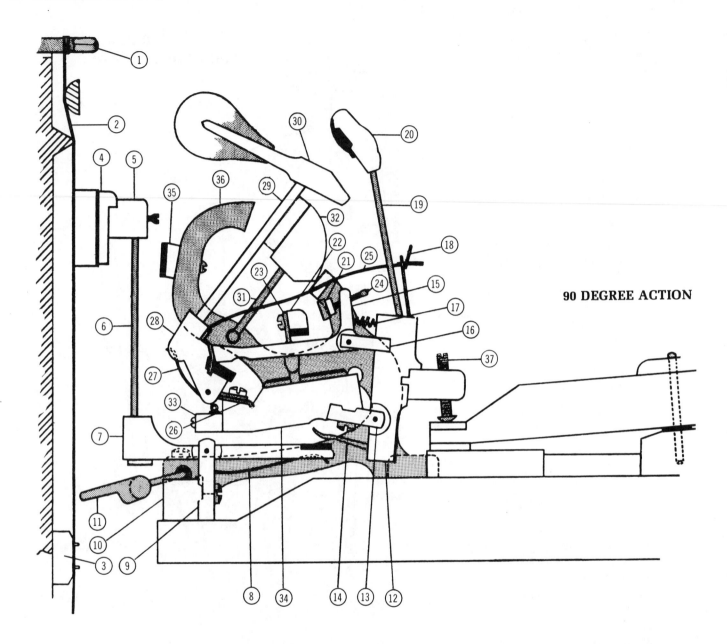

90 DEGREE ACTION

 1 *tuning pin*
 2 *string*
 3 *bridge*
 4 *damper*
 5 *damper head*
 6 *damper wire*
 7 *damper lever*
 8 *damper lever spring*
 9 *damper lever flange*
10 *action flange rail*
11 *damper rod*
12 *wippen*
13 *wippen flange*
14 *spoon*
15 *jack*
16 *jack flange*
17 *jack spring*
18 *bridle wire*
19 *back check wire*
20 *back check*
21 *let-off button*
22 *regulating rail*
23 *rail support*
24 *regulating rail screw*
25 *bridle tape*
26 *butt flange*
27 *butt spring*
28 *hammer butt*
29 *hammer shank*
30 *hammer*
31 *hammer rail support*
32 *hammer rest rail*
33 *butt knuckle*
34 *butt rail*
35 *damper stop rail*
36 *action bracket*
37 *capstan screw*

Table of hammer blow regulation

1-23/64 in.	Krakauer 37 in., 38 in., 40 in.	
	Haddorf 37 in., 38 in., 40 in.	
1-9/16 in.	Gulbransen	
1-5/8 in.	Acrosonic	Starck
	Cable Nelson	Wurlitzer 37 in.
	Hamilton Upright Studio	Jesse French
	Heintzman Upright	Everett
	Janssen	Story and Clark Drop Action
	Kimball 36 in.	
1-45/64 in.	Krakauer 45 in.	
1-3/4 in.	Lester ''Betsy Ross''	Sterling
	Cable (Conover)	Story and Clark Console
	Hardman	Weaver
	Ivers and Pond	Winter
	Kimball 38 in., 41 in., 45 in.	Wurlitzer 40 in., 44 in.
	Laughead	Weber
	Mason and Hamlin	Steck
	Henry F. Miller	Knabe
	Poole	Fischer
	Shoniger	Estey
	Sohmer Direct Blow	Chickering
1-7/8 in.	Baldwin Grand	Kranich and Bach
	Heintzman Grand	Sherlock-Manning
	Kimball Grand	Sohmer Drop Action
	Kohler and Campbell	Wurlitzer Grand
2 in.	Sohmer Grand	

Lesson 5 How to test the tune of a piano

If you were to place a long clothesline between two posts under tension, and then pluck it, you would notice that the vibrating body of the line would move in various ways. There would not be just one simple movement. The complete line would move in the form of an arc between the two bearing points.

In the piano, the wire moves in the same manner, and thus gives forth the fundamental prime tone. However, if one observed the vibrating clothesline, one would find that there were other movements which, when they occur in a piano string, set up different notes. These different notes are dependent on the length of the individual portion of the string which is moving. These notes are called harmonics. Some tuners call these overtones, while others call them both overtones and undertones. Keeping this in mind, we find that the note of C, the sixteenth note up from the bottom of a piano keyboard (piano keys are numbered from 1 to 88, moving from the bass to the treble) has a series of partial tones which work out as follows:

C (16): First partial

C (28): Second partial (one complete octave, or 12 keys up from the first note sounded)

G (35): Third partial tone (5 keys up from the second partial)

C (40): Fourth partial; middle C (a fourth up from the third partial)

E (44): Fifth partial (a major third up from the fourth partial)

Fortunately, the primary note usually sounds the strongest, and thus enables us to tune a piano. However, the tuner must keep constantly in mind the "partial tones" which are beating within the instrument as he tempers the scale and tunes throughout the piano.

The portions of the string which mark the point at which one movement stops and the next sectional movement begins are called *nodes*. While at least this much on the theory of sound must be mastered if one is to understand the basic vibrations which are keyed to the ear of the tuner, it is not intended at this time to go into a prolonged discussion of theory. Such study in depth will be a continuous part of this text, and tied in, wherever possible, with actual tuning practices. Thus, theory may be more easily learned and put to practical use while tuning.

What is vital at this point is that the reader understand that not just one tone is beat out by a piano string, but rather, a composite tone is produced which is made up of the partials just mentioned, and, in the process of tuning, an interaction between the fundamental tones, the partials, of one string and the fundamentals and partials of another some distance up or down the musical scale will be heard.

Muting the piano

In order to practice listening to these sounds, we first must mute the piano. There are usually three strings per note on the piano, ranging from the top of the bass to the extreme treble. Many tuners use two rubber wedge mutes, one placed at each side of the three string unison to be sounded, so as to cancel out the sound of the two outside strings. For reasons which will be easily understood, this practice will not be followed in this text. Rather, we shall mute the complete center section with the 52-in. felt muting strip. Not only will this mute all the strings in the temperament section, but it will have the added advantage of reducing the confusion from partial tones which we will be forced to deal with as we move out from the tempered section and begin to tune up and down the piano into other sections. We place the muting strip in the piano in the following way:

Beginning at the first treble string (which is a three-string unison), place the long rubber mute wedge on the string nearest the bass to deaden it. Now, using the handle of a rubber mute or a fine-bladed screwdriver, begin pushing the wide portion of the muting strip between the outside strings of each unison as you move up the piano, leaving a small loop of over 1/8 in. standing out from the center

Note the placement of the muting strip along the center section of the piano. This allows accurate temperament setting and proper control of octave unisons, as well as testing of intervals.

string. Continue doing this until you have used up the entire muting felt, with the thinner section being toward the right as you progress up the piano.

For more advanced students of piano tuning, an explanation may be helpful: Obviously, it is easier to differentiate between two sounds when the random overtones are at their minimum. To try to set a temperament with the use of rubber mutes per unison, and then to attempt to tune with open strings, three in number, beating against the single string you are trying to tune up or down the piano, is to complicate your hearing problem unnecessarily. There are tuners who tune well with rubber mutes, muting only one unison at a time, and then moving on, but they tune well in spite of the additional noise they are causing to impinge upon their ears. Therefore, the author finds that strip muting is the logical and practical answer for both beginning and advanced tuners.

Listening to the beats   Now, strike the notes in this temperament section all the way up until you run out of muted unisons. If any notes seem sour, mark the tuning pins which control those wires with chalk. If any hammers strike the mute strip of block against it, move the strip up or down so as to leave room for the main center string to be struck by the hammer. Place a short tip on your tuning lever (tuning hammer), and place the tip firmly upon the string pin so that it cannot rock. A snug fit is essential.

Carefully lift the fold of muting strip from one outside string in the center of the piano. Strike the strings with the hammer by depressing a key. Normally, you will hear two or more separate tones sounding at the same time. If these two tones are nearly at the same frequency, they will vibrate in such a way as to produce beats. For example, if the center string is at 523 cycles per second, it is moving the air at that speed. If the outside string is at 521 cycles per second, it likewise is moving the air at that speed. So there are two beats per second coming to your ear as the two strings vibrate together. One sound is overtaking the other twice in one second. At one instant, the movement is such that the sounds cancel each other out, and this is a null or quiet point. With the tuning lever held as nearly straight up and down as possible, move the pin on one string slightly to your left. The beats will change, since one string is going flat in comparison to the other.

If there is to be any change in the manner of holding the hammer, favor holding it so as to incline the end of the handle toward the bass. This gives a lift with the string when the hammer is moved, instead of a pull against the tension. Sound the tone again, and move the hammer to the right so as to lift the frequency of the string. Slight movements are always best. Move it in this direction until the beats slow down and disappear. This is zero beat or a quiet unison between the two strings. Continue moving to the right until the beats return and you are now on the up side of the unison, with the string sharp to the untouched string. With a slight pressure of the palm on the tuning lever, let the string down until the beats stop and your unison is again beatless.

At this time, we are not setting temperament nor worrying about the relative tune of one part of the piano as compared to another part. We are practicing the most essential part of piano tuning, which is learning to hear the actual beats between strings and to control the tuning lever at all times. You will note that often a unison will sound just fine until you release the pressure on the tuning lever, and then it will go flat, or in fewer cases, sharp. Remember that the string is being held by the upper bearing bar. The portion of string between the upper bar and the tuning pin is being pulled in such a way as to cause the remainder of string to slip a little up through the tensioned area at the bearing bar.

Naturally, there is more tension remaining between the pin and bearing bar than there is in the speaking length of the string. Furthermore, there is tension at the bridge which is tending to keep the speaking length from moving in exact accordance with the motions of the tuning pin. Practice in this area, lifting the tension and causing the beats to increase from flat to flatter, then to decrease as you bring the string up to unison, and then to hit the null point. From that point, move on up to a slow increase in beat rate as you go sharp to the unison, and lightly let the string down again.

It will take several hours of practice in this moving of unisons before you will be in sufficient control of the strings. Without sufficient control, no temperament setting is possible. With the aid of the clock, learn to space beats until they are 1, 2, 3, 4, 5, 6, 7, 8, 9, 10 per second. Spend some hours on this, as a sure sense of the speed of these beat rates is the key to proper tuning.

For variety, try setting the notes which are 12 hammers apart so that they sound the same tone, but exactly one octave higher or

The proper placement of the tuning lever on a pin in a vertical or upright piano allows maximum control without pulling against the tension of the string. Notice that the little finger is resting on the upper surface of the piano, while the tuning lever is gripped lightly with the fingers, which allows you to gently push and pull the lever.

lower. Use the unison beat system, swinging from flat to sharp, and lowering to quiet, just as in working with a single unison.

As you practice, you will find that certain positions of the hand and arm seem to make using the tuning lever easier. There are various schools of thought on this. Some insist that the unsupported arm is the only way one can tune, with the line of force moving from the lower back, up through the shoulder, then to the wrist and controlling the tuning lever. Others hold equally strongly to the idea that only the wrist and hand should control the lever. Still others feel that the elbow should serve as a fulcrum point for the lower arm and wrist to influence the precise movement of the tuning lever. Some tune left-handed exclusively. And still others say there is not sufficient control for a right-handed man when he tunes with the left, less controllable arm.

Since people come in different sizes, and pianos do, too, and pins are at different tensions, while dexterity of hand and arm are factors to be considered as well, the author will not impose his own method on those who tune pianos. Excellent tuning is being done both by left-handers and right-handers. It is also being done by those who support the elbow, and by those who use the unsupported arm.

The main objective is that you find for yourself the methods of approaching the tuning lever which enable you to control the movement of the pin and string with the greatest possible precision. We are working with fine units of single and fractional beats per second.

Try every way you can to discover which methods work best for you on different pianos. Each day, as a tuner, you will slightly modify your method in the interest of greater accuracy. There are only a few general guides which will never fail you. These are: Keep the hammer (lever) in a position corresponding to 10 o'clock to 12 noon whenever possible, for reasons which become increasingly clear as we continue tuning a piano. Do not pry upward or downward with any great force on the tuning pin while turning it. And keep sounding the tone by repeated firm blows of two fingers on the key while manipulating the string. We shall not tune pianos by turning tuning pins!

Keep your mind on the total length of string which must move over all its pressure points, and use the tuning pin as one portion of the total manipulation required to move it. The striking force of the hammer is another portion, and the release of friction points while tuning is still another. There are various standards of pitch. Up until about 27 years ago, there was one basic standard, called international pitch. While most old uprights were originally designed with the scale based on this pitch, you will be able to raise them to the new standard, A-440, or concert pitch, if the pins are reasonably tight and the strings are not weakened by rust or poor tuning practices. Actually, pitch refers to the vibrations per second of A above middle C, or key 49, counting up from the bass end of the piano. Middle C, or key 40, is set as a perfect octave down from key 52 which is set at 523.3 to correspond to A-440 in concert pitch, and to 517.3 when tuning in old international pitch. International pitch A equals 435.

When in doubt, tune the old piano to its original pitch, since the scale will usually sound better and more mellow. There are tuners who will argue with this approach, but it is difficult to prove logically why a piano designed and scaled for international pitch will be improved by raising the pitch to a standard which does not fit the scale design.

When preparing a piano to be played with an instrument which has a fixed intonation, such as an accordion or certain horns, it is better to raise the piano to A-440. But, in all cases, be guided by the condition of the pin tightness and the apparent age or weakness of the strings. New pianos and those recently made should all be tuned to A-440, and in some cases will be desired even higher (at A-442) for some concert artists. The pianos will stand it. Whenever raise in pitch of a quarter tone, or more, is required, two or more tunings will be needed to get tensions equalized, and make the piano stand in tune.

Even when tuned several times, a piano will not stand in tune unless the pins are properly set. To understand this and to accomplish proper pin setting, we must think about the total tension concerned in moving the string and pin. If one were to drive a tuning pin into the drilled hole of a piece of pin block material, and place an indicator on the upper and lower ends of the pin, one would see that even though the tuning lever causes a slight movement at the point of torque, there is no movement in the pin imbedded in the pin block. Therefore, we may assume that when one turns the top of a pin, he develops a twist or torque within the body of the tuning pin itself. This is caused by the strong frictional adhesion of the pin sides to the end plies of wood which surround it.

This torque, no doubt, will be extended throughout the pin, and in slightly different measure from its top to bottom. In addition to this,

The tuning lever may be manipulated by the left hand. A somewhat more comfortable position and more careful control of string tension are possible with this method. The hammer is set at an 11 o'clock position, which allows you to lift the string when raising the pitch, and to relax the pressure when lowering the pitch. Note that the hammer is held as closely as possible to the tip end so as to "feel" the setting of the pin and to give maximum control in tuning.

when the pin top is turned, the three coils of wire which surround it are changed slightly in their configuration around the tuning pin. Also, the portion of string which descends from the coils to the agraffe or upper bearing bar is caused to be pulled rather strongly in comparison to the longer speaking length of the string. This additional essential tension is relieved at the instant the speaking length begins to move through the agraffe.

The speaking length itself terminates at the bridge, where the down bearing and the side bearing of the bridge pins cause a slight binding of the string. This leaves the speaking length more highly stressed than the length behind the bridge until such time as the string creeps over it, and equalizes the tension from speaking length to hitch pin. It is imperative that the tuner, in order to have a solid tuning, arrange tensions so that the complete string has moved. In addition, he must relieve any torque he has set up in the pin before moving on to another string, since the slow or sudden release of such torque will lessen the tension between pin and bearing bar, and allow movement, however small, in the speaking length, and thus put the string out of tune. This process of applying torque and manipulating the string is referred to by tuners as "setting the pin." But it consists of much more than just setting the pin.

Setting the pin   Over the years the author has observed three commonly used methods to equalize the tensions existing in the tuning process. The first might be called the "wrench and pound" method. The tuner strikes the key, energizes the string, and instantly begins to turn the pin, downward at first, in old pianos, to loosen the friction points and to avoid string breakage, then upwards past the point of resonance, and slightly down to the desired pitch. While the tuner wrenches the pin back and forth, he vigorously strikes the key, so as to induce all possible movement in the various portions of the string and to avoid frictional hang-ups at any point. In addition, his vigorous pounding, which approximates the strongest blows a player will give the piano, helps prevent later stretching of the string by the pianist, and thus aids in establishing a rather firm tuning.

The second method is called "bend and kink." With this method, the tuner tries to avoid turning the tuning pin. Instead, he sets the string in motion as outlined previously, and by lifting on the pin, attempts to bring the string up through the pressure points. He then slightly lowers the overall tension by bearing outward on the handle of the tuning lever so as to lower the pin into the bottom of the tuning pin hole. By avoiding tuning pin wrenching, tuners prolong the life of the pin block, and, if successful in lifting the string, should establish a rather firm tuning.

With both methods, the tuner usually finishes his work on a string by giving it one hard "test blow" which, theoretically, knocks out any residual tensions yet unequalized, and also sets the pitch. This method avoids setting up strong torque in tuning pins, and thus prevents the sudden release of tuning pin torque, which can cause a piano to go quickly out of tune.

The third method is called "hopeful setting." With this method, the tuner, either by wrenching the pin or by bending it (for that is what happens when one bears heavily upward or downward upon a 10-in. tuning lever), gets the string to arrive at a point which is about one beat per second above the desired pitch. He then leans on the pin lever in the direction he wishes the string to go, either by laying the tuning lever at a 9 o'clock position, or by pushing it in that direction. He then strikes the string repeatedly by means of the piano key and action until the string drifts down to the pitch he desires. This method is assumed to relieve any residual tension in the pin, and at the same time, by use of the repeated blows, causes the string to be set in motion across the pressure points, and thus equalizes its fragmentary tensions. Hopefully, the string will not move farther downward after the hammer is removed from the tuning pin. But there is no way this can be guaranteed.

The author has perfected his own method, based on the salient tension equalizing and pin torque reducing practices which are found in the three discussed. His method should enable the beginner to tune pianos and to service them with professional skill. No matter what method one uses, he must always keep his objective in mind, and he must practice. Remember to maintain an overall concept, and try always to achieve it.

Bear the following important points in mind:
- Turning the pin establishes a torque in the body of the pin.
- The upper part of the string will originally be under greater tension than its speaking length.
- The string must move in its entirety during tuning, if it is to move over the bridges.
- Pianists strike the piano at least as hard as you do when you tune.

It is helpful, also, to remember that in the factory-tuned piano, the strings have been stretched possibly four times, and often many more times in high quality instruments. They have been positioned at concert pitch or better at the factory, and this has established certain curvatures and tension points in their lengths. The closer one comes to reproducing the original configuration of the strings in the piano, the more likely it is that the strings will not "creep" and that the tuning will remain solid.

To attempt to make a radical change in the positioning of the strings is to throw out of alignment many of the configurations which factory preparation has brought about. It is not wise to lift strings far above their standard pitch, because the upper length is then under greater pressure than usual; in effect, you are "cold working" the metal in the strings as it curves around the pin and as it passes under the upper bar or through the agraffe. In other words, you should let the piano work with you toward a firm tuning if you assume that somebody tuned it once before to its proper pitch and that the tensions set up at that time caused configurations in the strings.

A well-designed piano helps the tuner tune. Once you have tuned it well, you can establish your own "touch" in the piano. Future tunings will be a matter of resetting the strings so as to re-establish the tensions you last put into the piano. Over-stretching the strings tends to weaken them at pressure points; there is no "re-fattening" a string which has been elongated at one point in its total length!

Learn to handle the tuning lever delicately, and over the months you will find that the pads of your fingers become a secondary sensory point which, in addition to your ears, will enable you to "feel" a piano as you tune it. This business of piano tuning is more than a highly specialized skill. In every sense, it is an art. Treat it as such by being gentle with your use of tools and tuning lever, and the pianos will respond to your approach. Great strength is not a requirement in piano tuning; *controlled* strength most definitely is. Ideally one should have "the strength of a blacksmith and the delicate touch of a surgeon." This comes with practice and understanding.

Several hours should be spent each day in practicing unisons and in gently lifting and setting the pins before going to to the next chapter on temperament. Unless you master the skill of setting the string so that it stays where you put it, there is no point in learning temperament. If the temperament will not stay where you put it, all further efforts will be wasted. In addition, the time you require to tune a piano the first time can range from three hours to three days. Get this skill of pin and string setting to the point where you are a master and you will diminish your time on the first piano and on all others you tune. This is the most important skill you will master in piano technology. Many persons don't spend sufficient time to understand it, let alone practice it, to become good, solid tuners.

Close the C unison which you have been using for practice and open the left-hand string of A, key 37 on the piano. Now take the A-440 fork and strike it firmly against the open palm of the hand. Place the tail of the fork on a wooden resonant surface so that the sound will be amplified. Do this a few times until you can hear the beating fork clearly. Strike key 37 on the piano (A) and listen to find out if the fork sounds a beat against the open string or if the beat is absent. If it is absent, the A on the piano is in tune with the fork.

Additional practice in unisons

Usually, you will hear a beat between the fork and the string. Gently lower the string until there is an increase in beats, or lift the string to the right until the beats stop. Now lift over farther until there are 2 beats per second sharp (in other words, on the right side of the null point). Move the string farther to the right until there is a sound like a machine gun firing in the distance. This will be about 7 beats per second. Time it with the clock. Then try repeating to yourself "From Chi-ca-go to New York." This is 7 beats per second. Do this over and over until you can hear it clearly as the beats occur between the fork and string. Now lower the string until there are absolutely no beats between the string and fork. Then strike key 33 (F) on the piano.

Place your tuning lever on the center string of F and move the string until there are no beats between the F and the A when they are sounded together. Then lower the frequency of the F until you once again can hear "From Chi-ca-go to New York." Strike the key briskly and firmly until this ratio of beats remains precisely 7 beats per second. Repeat this exercise a number of times. When successfully completed, you have set your first interval on the temperament, and have established a beat rate which will be used in checking many portions of the temperament as described in the next lesson.

Lesson 6 How to establish temperament on a piano

Tempering is the process of altering the intervals in a pure scale so that the instrument may be played in all possible musical keys without using more than the 12 steps to an octave. All keyboard instruments must be tempered, or have the steps between notes shaded, in order to seem to be in tune in all keys. In fact, all tempered instruments are slightly out of key in every key, but musically sound right when the scale within the octave is properly tempered.

We set the temperament by tuning a series of fourths and fifths and checking them by the beat rates of thirds. In tempering the piano, we *narrow* the fifths and *widen* the fourths. To begin, we select the octave from F 33 to F 45, an octave of 8 full steps which is divided into 12 intervals of half steps. We are spacing these 12 tones so that they will be in tune within themselves regardless of the pitch.

To accomplish this with the least possible effort and error, tune each interval perfectly beatless, and then lower or raise the space between them as you have just done in the practice outlined in the preceding lesson. Remember to use the firm test blow while setting the pin so as to avoid confusion in your tempering if a note drifts.

It is possible to get the beats on the wrong side of pure resonance, and that is why practice in setting beatless unisons should be a constant accompaniment to your early trials at temperament. The tests which are outlined as we go along in the temperament will enable you to quickly and accurately tell if you have done something wrong, so don't become unduly worried. Mute all the center section of the piano as previously instructed, and you will be ready to begin.

Setting a C temperament from F to F

Tune the C above middle C, or key 52, to the fork at 523.3 beats per second. Tune down one octave and set middle C at a perfect beatless octave with the note above just tuned. (Work on center strings only.) Tune this interval over again until it remains perfect. Tune the F below middle C to a beatless interval with C. Then raise the pitch of F until it beats 3 times in 5 seconds sharp.

Tune the F above middle C to a beatless octave with the lower F. (Test: Strike middle C and the F above it. The beat rate will be 6 beats in 5 seconds. Test: Strike middle C and lower F. The beat rate will be one-half as fast.)

Tune A# to the upper F. First make it perfect, then sharp by 4 beats in 5 seconds. (Test: Strike A# and upper F. The beat rate will be the same as the interval from A# down to lower F.)

Begin intervals which are all tuned flat from resonance

Tune G below middle C to a beatless interval with middle C. Now flatten G until there are 4.4 beats flat in 5 seconds.

Tune D above middle C to G so that it goes perfect and then flat by 3.3 beats in 5 seconds. (Test: Strike A# and D. This should be a pleasant tremolo which is 9.2 beats per second. Test: Strike F and D together. The beat rate should be 8 per second.)

Tune A below middle C to D. Perfect, then flat by 1 beat per second. (Test: Strike lower F and A together. Beat rate 7 per second.)

Tune E above middle C to A. Perfect, then flat by 3.7 beats in 5 seconds. (Test: E down to G. Should be 8.9 beats per second. Test: E to C. Should be 10.4 beats per second.)

Tune B to E. Perfect, then flat by 5.5 beats in 5 seconds. (Test: Strike G and B together. Should beat at 7.8 beats per second.)

Tune lower F# to B. Perfect, then flat by 4.2 beats in 5 seconds. (Test: Strike F# and A# together. Should beat at 7.3 times per second. Test: F# and A# beat just slightly faster than F and A.)

Tune C# to F#. Perfect, then flat by 3.1 beats in 5 seconds. (Test: A and C# should beat 8.7 times per second together. Check with A# and D; the beat rate should increase by 0.5 beat per second.)

Tune G# to C#. Perfect, then flat by 4.7 beats in 5 seconds. (Test: G# to C beats 8.3 times per second. Test: F to G# and G# to upper F should beat the same.)

Tune D# to G#. Perfect, then flat by 3.5 beats in 5 seconds. (Test: A# to D# should beat a little faster than 1 beat per second. F# to D# should beat at 8.4 times per second.)

Now, test the temperament by starting with lower F and A. The beat rate should be 7 *beats per second*. Proceed up the temperament using this same interval of three keys between lower and upper notes. The beat rate should progress smoothly as you go up the scale in thirds by approximately 0.5 beat per second.

Here are some facts to keep in mind when trying to set a temperament: There are people who may try to tune a piano with the unaided sense of pitch, which they think would accurately split the eight-note octave into 12 equal steps. While a good exercise, this can never be as accurate as using the beat rate to accurately space and temper the octave. It is extremely doubtful that the unaided human ear can divide by one semitone. Even if this were accurately done, the tempering of the scale would still be required in order for the piano to play in tune in all 12 keys.

Do not cultivate a sense of musical pitch. The beat rates are the only possible way to do this temperament right. Remain calm if all the test intervals do not come out at precisely the beat rates you seek. Various pianos will perform differently. This accounts for the difficulty in tuning some smaller pianos, with string scales which are not uniform; and you often find that the beat rate of test intervals will not be exactly what you expected. Obtain the even progression of thirds and sixths from the bottom to top of your temperament. If you have to widen some intervals to get these beat rates progressing smoothly, do so.

Where narrowing is required, be guided again by the beat rates for thirds and sixths. The fourths and fifths are for establishing temperament only. The thirds and sixths are for fine-honing the temperament and precision work. Do not start with thirds and sixths, thinking you will check with fourths and fifths, because you will have used up your only micrometer measurement for fine tuning. And you will have no way of smoothing out your intervals.

In fact, once you have honed the temperament with thirds and sixths, you may find that the fourths and fifths beat at practically the same rate throughout your setting. If anything, the fifths will be only slightly slower, and usually the beat rate per fourth or fifth is very near to 1 beat per second. Fifths may be allowed to beat slightly faster than specified, and fourths can be allowed to beat slightly slower. The temperament you have just practiced is the basic tuner's temperament and will work out almost exactly as specified in fine grand pianos. With practice, it will approximate specific dimensions on 80% of the pianos you tune. Memorize it, use it, and trust it. When all else fails, this temperament will do the job.

Pertinent thoughts on temperaments: After a little experience, it becomes apparent that the fast-beating intervals cannot be heard and measured accurately except in comparison with each other. On the other hand, the basic beat of the tremolo can become a part of the tuner's experience and will give a good starting guide in checking all beats. Beat rates per second are a part of the tuner's mind which can come only with some months of intensive practice.

To instill a sense of the intervals of rough fourths and fifths in your consciousness, it might be helpful to imitate the cuckoo clock. A downward fourth is just about the interval of sound a cuckoo makes from the top note to the bottom one. Mechanically, the fourths are made up by leaving four hammers at rest between the notes being played. The fifths leave six hammers between the notes being played. The major third leaves three hammers at rest, and the sixth leaves eight hammers at rest between notes.

Numbering the keys

In a book such as this one, which deals with pianos from the tuner's view, you will find that all keys are numbered from the bottom left end of the keyboard, beginning with 1 and continuing upward to the extreme treble and ending with 88. Furthermore, all black keys are called *sharps* by tuners, although musicians refer to them as either sharps or flats, depending upon the key in which they are playing. For example, there are eight C keys on a piano. Their numbers are as follows: 4, 16, 28, 40, 52, 64, 76, 88.

Bear in mind that, with different standards of pitch for starting the temperament, there will be a slight change in the beat rates of individual intervals and temperaments. Again, steady progression of thirds and sixths is the only precise yardstick which will measure the accuracy of your temperament. The temperament or bearing of your scale must have smoothly beating increases in the thirds from the bottom to the top of your temperament.

The piano keyboard with the keys numbered and named in the center, or temperament area. The black keys (sharps) are numbered between the white keys (naturals).

Using an A# fork, or tuning from the C fork down to F and then up to A# to establish your beginning pitch, set the A# solid.

Tune F 45 up a fifth from A#. (Test: Play the octave F 33 to F 45.)

Tune C 40 down a fourth from the top F. (Test: Play F 33 and C 40 together, using previous tests.) Note: At this point you have developed two fifths which match each other. You have also developed two fourths which match each other.

Tune down from C to G. (Test: G to A#, slightly more than 10 beats per second.)

Tune from G to D. Set as in other temperaments. (Test: A# to D, 9.2 beats per second.)

Tune down from D to A, an interval of a fourth, remember? (Test: F 33 and A 37 should beat 7 times per second.)

Tune from A to E, up a fifth. (Test: C and E, beating slightly more than 10 per second. Should be similiar to the test between G and A#.)

Establish a temperament using A# as a starting pitch

Tune down from E to B, a fourth. (Test: Test with G and B; should beat 7.8 per second.)

Tune down from B to F#, which is the interval of a fourth. (Test: Play F# and A# together; should be 0.5 beat per second faster than F and A together.)

Tune up to C#, which is a fifth from F#. (Test: Play A and C# together; should be 8.7 beats per second.)

Tune down from C# to G#, which is a fourth. (Test: Play G# and C, which should be 8.3 beats per second.)

Tune up from G# to D# and set the fifth interval. (Test: B and D# together beat 9.8 per second.)

How to establish a good A temperament

Set up A 49 with the A 440 fork. Drop down an octave, and tune A 37 to the octave interval. Go up from A 37 to E, tune perfect, then flatten 1 beat per second. Drop down from A 37 to F 33, tune perfect, then set up 7 beats per second. Tune up from F 33 to A#38, which is an interval of a Fourth, tune to perfect resonance then raise A# to .8 beats per second sharp.

Go up from F 33 to C 40, tune perfect, then lift 1 beat per second. (Test: C to E should beat slightly over 10 beats per second.)

Go down from C to G, tune perfect, then flatten 1 beat per second. (Test: G to E should beat 8.9 beats per second.)

Tune up from G to D, perfect, then flatten 1 beat per second. (Test: F 33 to D should beat 8 beats per second.) (Test: Strike F 45 and A#, then F 33 and A#, the beat rate will be the same going to either F from A#38.)

Go down from D to A, and check to make sure the interval beats as a fourth. Tune from E to B, perfect, then flatten 1 beat per second. (Test: G to B should beat 7.8 times per second, or nearly the same as the interval from F to D.)

Tune down from B to F#, perfect, then flatten slightly under 1 beat per second. (Test: F# to A# equals 7.3 beats per second.)

Tune up from F# to C#, perfect, then flatten 1 beat per second. (Test: C# down to A equals 8.7 beats per second.)

Tune F 45 one octave up from F 33. (Test: C# up to F 45 equals 11 beats per second. Test: C 40 to F 45 equals less than 1 beat per second flat.)

Tune down from C# to G#, perfect, then flatten 1 beat per second. (Test: G# to C equals 8.3 beats per second. Test: F 33 to

G# same rate as G# to F 45, equals 9.4 beats per second.)

Tune up from G# to D#, perfect, then flatten a little less than 1 beat per second. (Test: D# down to F# equals 8.4 beats per second. Test: D# down to B equals 9.8 beats per second.)

Now, beginning at F 33 and A 37, make sure the first third beats at 7 beats per second (6.9) and that all thirds coming up from that point increase beat rate by 0.5 beat per second. Test a sixth from F to D and establish the 8 beats per second rate which should occur when you play G and B together. G# to C should give almost half a beat per second increase over G to B. Actual beat rates in minor thirds should be the same as the beat rates in major sixths (9.4 beats per second). For those who are not familiar with the keyboard, and for reference when setting temperament, an illustration is provided with keys numbered and named on the keyboard temperament section.

As you can see from a thorough study of temperaments just outlined, it doesn't much matter what key you start on, provided you get the beat rates progressing correctly in your total bearing. Forks are usually made in the keys suggested, but can be ordered in any pitch within the temperament.

Tuning by the multiple-fork method

At this point, it might be in order to answer a question which often arises as to why a person should not buy a complete set of 13 tuning forks and set the temperament which they would provide. A person could. However, no two pianos are the same in the harmonic interplay of the overtones and harmonics of their scales. Therefore, it would be next to impossible to get a musician's temperament on various pianos unless one were to control the humidity and temperature of each instrument and make sure they were precisely alike. Furthermore, having listened to quite a number of pianos which have been tuned in this manner by home tuners who were trying to save money, the author cannot agree that they were tuned properly. The fact that a competent tuner must be called to restore the instrument to playing condition is sufficient evidence of failure of the multiple-fork method.

Establishing a temperament and developing the proper beat rates within it are the marks of a careful and conscientious craftsman. Incompetents do not belong in the profession, since they are unable to cope with the various problems which arise when a piano is not perfectly scaled. And few pianos are perfectly scaled, due to limitations of space for string lengths, and to mechanical limitations of wire and sound board construction. In learning to set temperaments: "The hard way is really the easy way, and the easy way becomes the hard way."

When beginning tuners start a temperament, the use of the single fork is sufficient, but with the passing of time, and the addition of tuning skills, the craftsman wants to have a finer control, not only of his beat rate, but of his original pitch as well. To get closer control of the beginning note, it is a good idea to sound the fork and check the piano to see if it is near the pitch desired. Then play a third below the fork frequency and bring the lower note up to a recognizable beat.

Establish a steady beat rate for the third and then recheck the note which is to be aligned with the fork. For example, when setting a C temperament, if the beat between the G# and the C is pounded in at exactly the frequency desired, the piano key of C can be set at the same beat with the lower note and it will be absolutely on pitch.

While setting temperament, consider the fact that it would be difficult to set a clear beat temperament if the side strings on each unison were not muted by the muting strip. Some tuners try to mute each unison with two rubber wedge mutes, and having set the center string, they bring in the right and left strings and then proceed to set their next interval. This, it seems to me, invites increasing the possibilities of spurious harmonic beats which will make for a ragged temperament, and certainly not make the job any easier or better.

The best way is to mute the entire center section of the piano with a muting strip. Furthermore, when proceeding to tune the remainder of the piano to match the temperament, it is advisable whenever possible to mute the entire instrument, establish the complete tuning on the center strings (and on one string of each unison in the bass), correct the slippages which may occur on some strings, and then lift the side strings to pitch.

Besides avoiding the supreme error of tuning to harmonics, this method distributes the increasing tensions of the center strings evenly over the surface of the bridges, and thus to the sound board. In this way, one-third of the tension is applied uniformly throughout the instrument, and subsequent "chunking in" of outside strings is less likely to materially alter the temperament and the overall set of the piano.

In the lessons on tuning the piano beyond the temperament section, we will be testing with other intervals, such as tenths and seventeenths. This accurate form of checking, as one goes up and down the piano, is next to impossible with open unisons. Therefore, it is much better fitted to a complete muting of the piano while tuning. On fine grands, there is no question that full muting is the best possible way to fine tune. But on less expensive instruments, the poorer quality may lead to considerable trouble with harmonics, and thus disrupt your tuning. It is wise to strip mute the whole piano.

Ordinarily, one would suppose that moving out from the temperament would simply be a matter of setting octaves up and down the piano until all notes are in harmony with the temperament. Such is not the case, although certainly we must complete the tuning this way. However, we cannot count on the accuracy of the simple octave when we are tuning a piano. A completely beatless octave will still be shown to be in error when tested by thirds and sixths. And stretching the piano to accommodate both objective tuning accuracy and subjective musical tonality will be more beautifully done if we use intervals other than octaves.

The major third is the most precise control in tuning, both in temperament and in complete pianoforte revision. To use it, we must amplify its authority in places where it may beat in a manner we cannot hear, by using expanded multiples of the third. To do this, we will function better with a strip muted piano.

Lesson 7 Setting temperament with a Strobotuner

The Strobotuner is an electronic instrument which gives an accurate visual indication of the frequency of a sound or an electrical signal. It compares the frequency to be measured with internal frequency standards based upon the equally tempered musical scale, but can be used to measure frequencies in any scale. By stroboscopic comparison it indicates if the frequency being checked is sharp, flat, or in tune with the reference standard.

The range of the Strobotuner covers seven octaves or 84 half-steps in the scale. It extends from C1 (three octaves below middle C) to B 7 in ordinary operation. Its useful range actually extends beyond these limits as will be explained in the instructions.

For many years stroboscopic tuning devices have been used to calibrate the speed of rotating objects. Since most musical tones can be received by microphone and their frequencies can be contrasted with an inner standard frequency, it seems, at first thought, that the use of a strobe offers absolute accuracy when tuning temperament. Some tuners have gone so far as to state that they do not think it necessary to learn to set temperament by any other means.

Old-time tuners and technicians frown upon the unrestricted use of the stroboscopic apparatus in setting a piano because they feel that a mechanical device cannot take the place of the human ear and mind in laying out the bearings on a piano. Furthermore, it is just possible that some also fear that any Tom, Dick, or Harry who buys a

Strobotuner will rush out with more nerve than knowledge and proceed to abuse a great number of fine pianos. Often such is the case, especially among those who work at other occupations during the day and then try to tune pianos in their spare time.

The skills of piano craftsmanship are so varied, and the rewards so excellent in both a financial and emotional sense, that it is difficult to understand why men who enter the field do not proceed to become the finest technicians they can possibly be. Certainly there is adequate demand for their services, but shabby, fly-by-night attempts leave both the customer and the piano apprentice unhappy. Suffice it to say that the Strobotuner will never make a man a piano tuner. But a conscientious piano craftsman can use the well-engineered Strobotuner to become even more precise in his work. The instrument serves exceptionally well as an aid in tuning electronic organs, and no organ technician should be without one.

It is possible to calibrate the Strobotuner by using any standard frequency for any note of the musical scale. In addition, the instrument can be calibrated by switching to the internal 60-cycle-per-second sine wave which is transmitted through the AC power line. Complete calibration instructions come with the instrument.

An airborne microphone is standard equipment with the Strobotuner and it is usually used to pick up tones and to supply an electrical signal to the input signal receptacle. A contact microphone or a vibration pickup can be used instead of the airborne microphone, if desired. In some applications, such as tuning electronic organs, an electrical signal can be supplied to the input signal receptacle directly without the use of a microphone, if desired. The voltage of the signal supplied should be between 1 millivolt (1/1000 volt) and 1 volt.

Set the tone selector knob for the tone to be checked. If concert pitch is being used (as for a piano, or other instrument in C), the C on the knob is used as the indicator. The tone selector knob can be used as a transposing device also for instruments in the keys of B flat, E flat, or F. For example, when playing the note C (as written) on a B-flat instrument, the B flat on the tone selector knob can be set opposite C on the panel and the Strobotuner will be set for measuring the C (as written), which is A# (B flat) concert. Since keyboard instruments such as pianos, harpsichords, and organs are in the key of C, no transposition is involved between the written note and the tone sounded; thus the C on the tone selector knob is used as the indicator to line up with the appropriate letter on the panel.

THE STROBOTUNER

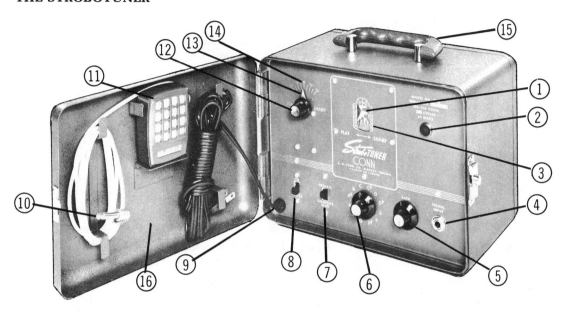

The Conn Strobotuner with controls numbered and identified. More elaborate instruments are also available.

1 scanning disc
2 pilot light
3 octave band numbers
4 signal input
5 gain control
6 tone selector knob
7 operate-calibrate
8 power switch

9 power cord
10 microphone plug
11 microphone
12 tuning knob
13 tuning pointer
14 tuning scale
15 carrying handle
16 cover

After the tone selector knob has been properly set for the tone to be tested, and the tone signal has been properly fed into the input signal receptacle, a stroboscopic pattern should appear on the scanning disc. If the tone being tested is between C 1 (32.703 cps) and B 1 (61.735 cps) the pattern will be on the band nearest the center of the disc (band 1).

Band Number	Frequency Range
1	C 1 (32.703 cps) — B 1 (61.735 cps)
2	C 2 (65.406 cps) — B 2 (123.47 cps)
3	C 3 (130.81 cps) — B 3 (246.94 cps)
4	C 4 (261.63 cps) — B 4 (493.88 cps)
5	C 5 (523.25 cps) — B 5 (987.77 cps)
6	C 6 (1046.5 cps) — B 6 (1975.5 cps)
7	C 7 (2093.0 cps) — B 7 (3951.1 cps)

If the tone being tested is in tune with the equally tempered tone at the pitch standard used to calibrate the Strobotuner, a stationary pattern will be seen for each tone produced. If a tone is flat (lower in frequency) to the equally tempered scale frequency, the stroboscopic pattern will rotate to the left. The speed at which the pattern drifts is an indication of how much it deviates from the equally tempered scale. If you wish to measure how flat the tested tone is, turn the tuning knob so its pointer moves to the left until the stroboscopic pattern becomes stationary. Then read the number of cents flat from the position of the pointer on the tuning scale. Similarly, if the tone being tested is sharp (higher in frequency), then the equally tempered scale frequency of the stroboscopic pattern will rotate to the right and it can be stopped by turning the tuning knob clockwise.

A simple flute-like tone tends to produce a sharper stroboscopic pattern generally and it will appear distinctly on only one band. If the tone being tested has strong upper partials, they will cause patterns to appear on the higher number bands also. For example, if A 2 (110 cps) is being tested, its second harmonic (220 cps) may cause a pattern to appear on the third band from the center of the scanning disc, and its fourth harmonic (440 cps) may cause a pattern in the fourth band, and so on for octave-related harmonics.

If the partials in a tone being tested are not whole number multiples (harmonics) of the fundamental frequency, it will be possible to get a stationary pattern for the fundamental of the tone (its lowest frequency) while the patterns formed by the higher partials are drifting. *This will be true generally for piano tones or chime tones.*

In discussing the use of the Strobotuner with experienced tuners who are devoted to the aural method of tuning, I find the principal complaint they have is that the pianos they service which had previously been tuned by someone with a strobe were not tuned so that the beats within the temperament were according to standard aural measurements. Whether this condition is due to poor understanding on the part of the strobe tuner of how to use this fine electronic instrument, or poor technique on his part in learning how to set the pins, the author cannot say. But certainly, after some years of experience with using Strobotuner methods and aural temperaments, he is in a position to state that it must be one or the other. It takes more than a frequency standard to properly set a temperament.

Without understanding harmonics and their properties, and without integrating the harmonic content of the piano while tuning, there can be no decent temperament or tuning. The Conn Corporation provides explicit instructions as to the compensations required for partial tones while tuning with the Strobotuner, and one cannot properly use the instrument without mastering the instruction book and practicing regularly with its teachings in mind. Furthermore, as previously explained in detail, unless one learns how to set the pin properly, no adequate temperament is possible. In other words, it appears that most Strobotuner tuners have not practiced their skills to the extent that aural tuners have.

The author knows of one tuner who uses the strobe and whose work is pleasing some of the most critical musicians in his area. The instrument cannot do for the tuner what the tuner will not learn to do well. But it can be a great tool when used as an aid to a conscientious craftsman.

To clarify matters for those who do not understand the Strobotuner, and to refresh the minds of those who may have skimmed over original instructions, the following information is offered:

Stretching the octaves

Many technicians prefer to start tuning at the "break" in the scale because of the marked change in the inharmonicity of the partials of the tones at this point. The stiffness of piano strings causes the tones produced to have partials that are not harmonically related to each other; that is, the second partial is not exactly twice the frequency of the first partial, or fundamental, of the tone. The third partial is not three times the frequency of the fundamental, and so on. For the partials to be harmonic they need to bear a whole number relationship (1, 2, 3, 4. . .) to the fundamental. The partials in piano tones are nearly always slightly higher (sharp) than the whole number multiples (harmonics) of the fundamental. This has a very important bearing upon the tuning of a piano.

When listening to two piano tones an exact octave apart, the second partial of the lower tone will be sharp with respect to the fundamental of the higher tone. This will cause audible beats to be produced and the listener will not consider the tones to be truly an octave apart even though the fundamental frequency of the top tone is exactly twice the fundamental frequency of the lower tone, as is required for a true octave. In order for the octave on the piano to sound in tune when the two notes are played at the same time, it is necessary to stretch the interval by lowering the bottom tone or raising the top tone. The technique for determining the optimum amount of stretch with the Strobotuner will be clearly explained as we go along.

The temperament octave

The inharmonicity of piano tone partials is usually smallest in the middle of the keyboard, so an octave is chosen there for setting the temperament. Usually care should be taken that the "break" or a marked change in string design does not occur within the temperament octave.

All but one string per key is muted with felt or wedges so only one string at a time sounds when a key is struck.

Tuning the treble strings

Let us assume that C 4 (middle C) is chosen for the starting point as an example. Some other starting point might be preferred and could be used as well. Proceed from C 4 up the scale, tuning one string on each key while watching the fourth ring or pattern band. The Strobotuner pointer remains in the position chosen to establish the tuning standard while tuning this octave.

It may be noted that while tuning this octave even though the tension on the string is adjusted to cause the fourth ring pattern to be stopped, the patterns in the fifth and higher rings will move slowly to the right due to the fact that the partials producing those patterns are not exactly in a 2, 4, 8, etc., relationship to the fundamental of the tone. If the fifth ring pattern moves to the right for the C 4 string when the fourth ring pattern is not moving, the tuner can note how far to the right he needs to move the Strobotuner pointer in order to make the fifth ring pattern stand still. If this is one cent or more, it indicates that C 5 should be tuned sharp by at least that amount. Therefore, when tuning C 5, the pointer is advanced to the right of the starting position used for tuning the temperament octave. This is the beginning of the octave stretching process.

It may be that the inharmonicity of the partials in the C 4 string is so small that it is negligible. If that is the case, the pointer should be left in the C 4 position while tuning C 5, and this octave is not stretched. Since inharmonicity of partials is caused by the stiffness or rod-like character of the strings, it is obvious the short, thick strings will have greater inharmonicity of their tone partials than will long slender strings. Therefore, the degree of inharmonicity will vary from string to string in a given piano and will vary between pianos. The degree of inharmonicity is greater at either end of the piano keyboard than it is in the middle, and it tends to be greater in small spinet pianos than in grand pianos.

As the tuner proceeds up the scale from the temperament octave, he gets a good idea of how much to stretch the octave by sounding the tone an octave below the one he is tuning and noting how sharp the second partial is with respect to the true octave. As he goes up the scale he will note a marked increase in this inharmonicity, and he finds that the higher he goes the more stretch is required in the octave. Due to the wide variety of piano designs, no set rule can be stated for stretching the octaves but the Strobotuner gives an accurate measurement of the condition that exists to guide the tuner so that he can tailor the stretch to fit each particular piano.

Optimum compromises

The fundamental is usually the strongest partial in the tones above C 4, and the higher partials are progressively weaker. Thus, the fundamental and the second partial are the two most important parts of the tone to consider when tuning octaves. However, the meticulous tuner may find that even though the fundamental is exactly in tune with the second partial of the tone a stretched octave below, some beating between tones exists. If such is the case, he is hearing beats between higher coincident partials, such as the fourth partial of the lower tone and the second partial of the higher tone.

These partials can be noted in the Strobotuner patterns at the same time the lower partials are indicated. Taking the fourth octave tones as an example, the fundamental is indicated in the fourth band, the second partial in the fifth band, the fourth partial in the sixth band, the eighth partial in the seventh band. Since the higher partials are relatively weak and die out quite rapidly after the tone is sounded, the patterns for the upper partials usually will not be as clear as the lower partial patterns.

If the tuner finds that objectionable beats exist when the fundamental is exactly in tune with the second partial of the tone, an octave below, he will note relatively strong patterns for the upper partials and can measure how much mistuning exists between the higher coincident partials. He can then stretch the octave even further by the amount needed to reduce the beats between the higher coincident partials. In so doing he introduces beats between the lower coincident partials, and therefore the resultant tuning must be a compromise which depends upon the degree of inharmonicity and the relative strength of the upper partials.

The degree of compromise is determined by the information revealed by the Strobotuner plus what the tuner *hears*. Compromise tuning is necessary because of the nature of piano tones and is not related to the method of tuning. It must be understood that the tuner does not "turn off" his ears while tuning with the Strobotuner, for it is quite important that he correlate the information obtained visually from the Strobotuner with the information he gains through hearing. The eyes and ears working together can give far more information than either can give alone.

As you can readily see, the designers of the instrument did not think it would automatically make anyone a piano tuner. The deft skills required to tune well are augmented by the use of a Strobotuner. It would be foolish indeed to maintain that the human ear will reasonably excel the combination of ear and eye together. Consider, if you will, the speed of sound which comes to and impinges upon the human ear. This speed is around 1,035 ft. per second. Now consider the speed of light and electricity which is about 186,000 miles per second. Which is likely to be more accurate?

In using the Strobotuner, the author has always found that, once the temperament is established, it is best to start checking the progression of musical thirds and sixths, as in the aural method, and to alter the harmonic content of the temperament so as to provide clean fifths, steadily progressing thirds, and beating sixths. From that point on, one may calibrate the strobe to match the temperament as just defined, and proceed to tune the entire piano by ear, or by strobe, using thirds to check his octaves while going up the piano or down. In addition, as one tunes beyond the normal audible beat rate in going up or down the piano, he should add an octave to his third, or sixth, and check his beat rates steadily as he goes along. In this way, he uses the best of both methods.

Of course, some persons may want to completely tune the piano with the Strobotuner. For them, a method is outlined in the Conn manual.

Tuning the bass strings

Return the Strobotuner pointer to its original starting position chosen for the tuning standard and proceed to tune downward from the string chosen as the starting point. When tuning in the third octave use the pattern in the fourth band rather than the one in the third band. This tunes the second partial of the third octave tone to the fundamental of the tone a stretched octave above it in the fourth octave.

When tuning the strings in the second octave the tuner can choose which band to use according to the strength of the partials in the tone as indicated by the clarity of the patterns. If the fourth band pattern is the most pronounced, the pointer is left in the same position as it was while tuning the third and fourth octave. This puts the fourth partial of the second octave tone in tune with the second partial of the third octave and the fundamental of the fourth octave. This often is the most satisfactory procedure.

In some cases the tuner may find it advantageous to use the third band patterns while tuning the second octave strings. If such is the case he will set the Strobotuner pointer at the position that causes the third band pattern to be stationary when sounding the third octave string previously tuned; then tune the second octave string to make the third octave band pattern stationary. This tunes the second partial of the second octave tone to the fundamental of the third octave tone.

The first octave is tuned in a manner similar to the second octave. Usually the third band is used for tuning the first octave after setting the Strobotuner pointer in the position that causes the third band pattern to be stationary when the previously tuned third octave string is sounded.

The fundamentals of the lower tones are generally very weak and have little influence on the tuning. This is indicated by their weak patterns on the Strobotuner. Since it is the stronger upper partials that are heard and are of concern to the tuner, he need not be concerned by the weak or missing patterns for the fundamentals of the lower tones. This fact is of importance also in tuning the bottom three strings since their fundamentals are below the range of the Strobotuner.

The tuner will quickly discover the best microphone placement and striking technique for obtaining the clearest patterns. On the highest tones, where the sustaining time is short, he may find that striking the key in rather rapid succession gives the best pattern.

It may be noted that if a key is struck in such a manner as to produce a loud tone, it is flatter immediately after being struck than it is during the remainder of the tone. This characteristic of the piano tone requires the tuner to make a choice as to whether the initial portion of the tone or the latter part is in tune. The difference is small enough that it is usually negligible.

There is no reason why there should be disagreement when tuners discuss the Strobotuner. Much of the excellent material presented in the manual is germane to all piano tuning, no matter what method is employed. The factual information regarding partial tones and their accurate calibration throughout the tuning process is enough in itself to make every piano craftsman want to own and to use a Strobotuner. It would improve his understanding of what takes place when he is tuning a piano. Furthermore, the excellent material presented in printed form by the Conn Corporation and their representative engineering seminars regarding inharmonicity of piano strings contributes a great deal to better piano technology.

A craftsman who reads their materials, which are developed in controlled laboratory surroundings, is bound to become a better tuner and technician. And much of what Strobotuner users can learn from their aural tuning colleagues can be paid for by the careful and responsible approach Conn suggests in their publications.

Digest what is included in this lesson, whether you intend to use an electronic tuning aid or not. The factors of partial tones and inharmonicity management in piano tuning are an integral part of your development as a tuner.

Lesson 8 Tuning the octaves up and down the piano

After setting the temperament, the completion of the tuning job is a matter of setting the octaves out of the basic notes of the temperament up and down the piano. Although we talk of going "up" and "down," in actual practice it seems that more consistent tuning is done in the reverse order. In other words, we begin at the top note of the temperament and then go down one octave to set the first note, proceeding from that point to go down another note to set the next octave, and so on throughout the bass of the piano.

There is a good reason for setting the bass first. As you will notice when viewing the piano, the bass section is in another wing of the casting, and the bass strings bear against a separate bridge and remote part of the sound board as compared to the tenor (middle) and treble (upper) tone strings. For this reason, changes in the bass do not cause as much upset in the over-all tension of the piano as do changes in the upper tenor and lower treble. So it is best to tune the lower end of the piano first, using one string to the unison in pianos which have three string unisons moving into the bass, then one string per unison in those unisons which have two bass strings, finally ending up with a single string tuning on the single bass strings. Usually it is best to set the E below middle C, then the D# below middle C, and continue on in this way. Then move down to the next octave and repeat the performance.

The first several tones in the bass, as you move down from the temperament, will be quite easy to get right, since they are not too sensitive, and you will be able to hear beats quite well. However, as you move down further toward the bass end, beats will be heard which will be difficult to select from in tuning. Start listening for a much lower beat which sounds like a deep-voiced frog croaking from some distance under the piano. This is the lower or fundamental beat. It is not the loudest beat you will hear, but it is easily recognizable and usable. Remember that most tones heard in the bass are the higher partials and harmonics. This will eliminate much confusion.

Tuning the bass   Added stiffness in the bass strings will make it necessary for you to always work on the lower tones you hear. In fact, stretching the bass consists of flatting the lower tones as you go down until they are satisfying to the human ear, and still nearly mathematically correct. In the larger, well-made pianos, the stretch may be only 4% to 5% flat. In smaller pianos, with their added inharmonicity factors and shorter, stiffer bass strings, the stretch required to make a tonally pleasing tuning can run as high as 10% flat. To make this stretch work out well, two useful techniques may be employed:

1. Strike the note which is to be used as your upper tone. Hit it with one quick blow and then immediately with a sustained blow. One-half second later, drop in the lower note to be tuned and, while holding both keys, adjust the lower note. Now strike the lower note quickly, then again immediately with a sustained blow. Half a second later, create a tone on the upper note the same volume as the lower note. This system works well.

2. After using the first method, start at the upper third above your top reference tone, add one octave coming down, then play the lower and upper notes together. You are now using a tenth. Play tenths right on down by half steps to your lower tone, keeping the upper and lower tones this far apart. You will be able to hear the smoothness or lack of it in the descending beat rate. When you reach a point going downward at which the reacting beats become too muddy to hear well, add another octave between the upper note (which is one-third above the octave note used as reference) with the lower note being tuned. You are now using a seventeenth.

Continue down through the bass with this method for accuracy. Do not tune with arpeggios. But after setting a bass tone, the lower note can be quickly checked by playing an arpeggio (tonic or first note of a chord, then down to the fifth, then the third, and using the lower note as bottom tonic of the chord). Any mistakes will easily be heard.

After setting the bass strings, you are ready to move upward from the temperament to the treble end of the piano. Use the octave note below the first untuned note as your reference. In other words, if you have established a good C temperament, with F above middle C as the top tone tuned in the temperament, begin your treble tuning with F# below middle C, sounding it and then sounding the untuned F# above middle C. Adjust the top note for a beatless octave with the lower one. Now, sound the third below middle C by using the lower F# reference tone and the D below middle C (which you have tuned while tuning the bass). Sound the third using the two same notes above middle C. Compare the beat rates. Are the beats doubling as you play notes one octave apart?

From this point, continue up the piano, a half-step at a time, until you have reached the top end note, which is C 88. In the first octave above the temperament, you will have little difficulty. But at the point where the "break" occurs in the treble scale, usually where the casting portions come up between the treble unisons and a wider space between unisons exists, you will find many harmonic beats which will be difficult to identify. Start tenths at this point.

As the scale discrepancies become more pronounced going upward, begin using both tenths and seventeenths to check the setting of your top note. Some false beats are caused by the music wire being twisted or kinked when the piano was strung. At this point, complete muting of the piano becomes really helpful, since it enables you to concentrate on one string at a time, and identifies the beats more clearly in your octave.

Always try to keep the upper tone on the upper edge of the resonance point as you tune upward. Again, you will be stretching the piano so as to arrive at a compromise between mathematical precision in an octave spread and musical tonality. Strike the treble with some force, since a minute change in tensions in this section will cause the greatest change in pitch. Now play an arpeggio up to each note being tuned as a final check. If the top note sounds either flat or sharp, correct it, and trust the musical tonality you hear. Do not tune by arpeggio. That way lies chaos.

Tuning the treble

When you use the arpeggio for testing the musical fitness of your octave, you are on solid ground, since you are sounding the tonic, the third, the fifth, and once again the top tonic note. You can hear the music. But to attempt to tune with this method is to defeat the beat ratio you set up in your temperament and to cause the piano to play well in only a few keys.

Once the single string of each unison has been properly tuned from bottom to top of the piano keyboard, you are ready to begin in the bass and to open the muted strings, then to tune them to a perfect beatless unison with the tuned string of that unison. In the main, completing the tuning of the piano will be only a matter of lifting the mute from a string, and tuning that string to the center string. Then, in three string unisons, tune the other side string to the beatless unison which exists between the two tuned strings you have just finished.

It is not a good idea to mute one side which has just been tuned while you are working on the third string of a unison. Of course, if you have not properly quieted the unison between the center and left-hand strings, it will make for more beats than you can alter with the right-hand string. But, if you get the left and center strings perfectly in tune with each other, you will find that you can more evenly harmonize a beatless unison by tuning the right string with the other two strings open and sounding. If there has been a shift in one of the two strings just tuned, you will quickly hear it, and also, you can often cancel out inharmonicity to some extent while tuning the third string to the unison. Continue up the piano until all strings in all unisons are beatless with the center strings you have just tuned.

In the upper treble, listen for a clear bell tone without echoes. You will hear a sudden drop in volume in the treble unison when you are "dead on." This is the null point where there is no "wang" in the unisons and is the ideal goal you are trying to reach.

Now, let us consider what you did when you completed this method of tuning. First, you laid the temperament on the center and most accurate section of the piano. Second, you moved out from there, tuning one string of each note only and thus laid a third of the additional tension upon the bridges and sound board (which will be the result of tuning the piano). You thus forestalled shifts in tension which could later occur if you just moved up a piano bringing in all three strings of each unison before moving on to the next note. Then you added the slight additional tensions of the left strings of the unisons and still kept the piano in reasonably equalized tension. Finally, you laid in the remaining third of the new tension, and the result was a piano whose overall tension pattern was not greatly disturbed throughout the tuning process.

When you are finished with the piano, do not ask the customer how he likes it. As far as you are concerned, it is a perfect job. If a piano student is present, you may ask him to play something for you. This enables you to hear anything that may be wrong. But, in every case, conduct yourself as a professional, and do not ask anyone's opinion of how the piano sounds.

The piano tuner as musician

Many piano tuners are fine musicians, but many are not even slightly musically inclined. It makes little difference when one is listening for beat rates. Sometimes it is a help to have a musical ear when touching up the octaves so as to have a piano stretch which will suit the discriminating musician. However, some of the finest concert tuners can play only "Tea for Two" when they are done with the job. The piano is not tuned by ear. It is tuned by beats. It is tuned by men who may differ in their opinions on how much stretch should be put into it, on proper tuning lever techniques, and on the merits of various makes of pianos.

But the piano is tuned so infrequently in most homes that the average householder doesn't know what a *tuned piano* sounds like. Some will say, "You took the 'wang' out of our piano," or, "It doesn't sound as loud as it did." Both statements are true, since the "wang" depends on unisons which are beating while differing by a few cycles per second within themselves, and the three strings sounding at slightly different tones in a unison seem to have more volume than a perfectly tuned unison. Don't worry; when a few days have passed, some "wang" will be back in certain notes. And on your first 200 pianos, there will be some "wang" a lot sooner than you'd expect.

The first piano tuning can take from two hours to two days. Every tuning thereafter will be faster, until, after several hundred pianos, you will probably be doing an acceptable job in 45 minutes to an hour. After 1,000 pianos, you will be taking longer, because you will not be satisfied with anything less than your best! Seldom will the accomplished tuner find a piano that sounds the way he thinks it should. When by fortuitous circumstance he is called to tune one and discovers a well-made, properly cared for instrument, his heart will beat faster and his eyes will glow. And on that day, as he tunes, he will thrill to the sounds and feel that he is the most fortunate of men. He may even come back to hear the instrument played by a good musician. He then will know how good he is at his profession.

At this point, review the proper pin setting methods outlined previously and practice beatless unisons, beating thirds and sixths until you are confident that mastery of this art can be yours. Keep in mind that there is more to making piano tone than just the tuning. Hammers, with their varying densities and thus undependable sounds; the composition of the hammer shank materials, graining, the alignment of the grains, the quality of action materials and their interference with the fluid flow of energy to the string, are all components of tone production. And so are the case design, sound board construction, bridge bearings, and scale design. Other instruction will be covered as we continue with this text.

The complete piano must be understood and its characteristics conditioned in the mind of the tuner if he is to get the best possible tone out of the instrument. But for now, at least, you should be able to tune a piano.

A review   Always tune one string of each unison from the top to the bottom of the piano. Setting the string is more important than anything else you do. Don't trust octaves: use thirds, tenths, and seventeenths in all your tunings.

Lesson 9 How to make pin and string repairs

Piano strings are made of music wire which comes in different sizes or diameters. Throughout the scale of a piano, the gradations of music wire from size 23 in the tenor up to size 13 in the high treble change every few unisons. Some pianos even go as high as size 12. It is essential to have a small micrometer or else a music wire gauge when doing string repairs on a piano. Actually it is preferable to buy an accurate, small micrometer rather than a music wire gauge, a tuning pin size gauge, a flange center pin gauge, etc. The micrometer is more accurate and considerably more useful, and in addition, usually costs about the same as all these other gauges combined.

Should you break a string while tuning, replace it from the point where it winds three turns around the tuning pin on through its complete length across the bridge, down around the hitch pin, up over the bridge again, and up to the next unison tuning pin. There is a method of tying a square knot in the piano string that breaks above the bearing bar. It saves time. Some technicians maintain that tying the broken part of the string allows you to tune it up to pitch or a little above and does not require the three tunings of this area which replacing with a new string would need. For those who wish to use this method, it is herewith outlined:

Use a pair of regular pliers, a pair of music wire cutters, and any long-nosed gripping tool available. Gauge the diameter of the broken string, and then either pry the "eye" of bent wire out of the tuning pin, or punch the coil with the coil punch, thus cutting the eye and freeing the coils around the tuning pin. Remove the coils.

Take some music wire of the same size as the broken string and make a loop at one end. Then make a loop at the top end of the broken string. Make one loop smaller than the other, and keep a gradual curve in the loops, without kinks or severe bends. Slip the smaller loop into the larger one and, leaving enough wire above the tuning pin to make three turns on the pin, cut the repair wire and insert it into the eye of the tuning pin.

Draw up the string until the square knot becomes tight and small. Usually loops made about 5 in. in length will suffice. Of course, you use the string lifter to lift the coils so as to get a uniform setting around the tuning pin. Space the repaired string in its unison according to the spacing of the other unisons in the piano.

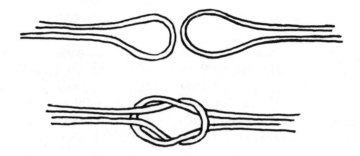

REPAIR LOOP OF STRING

The author favors replacement of the complete string in repair. Even though it may be necessary to tune it two or three times, you have improved the piano rather than patched it. Besides, the old string may break again due to age and deterioration at another point. Always leave a piano in better condition than when you found it.

In the matter of bass strings, a rapid repair method is not so easily found. Bass strings are wound strings and their precise winding is a significant part of their response properties. When a bass string is broken, it is better to send the string to either the manufacturer or the supply house. When removing the string, note its position in the piano, using only the key number which affects it. In other words, do not say, "E string, two octaves below middle C." Do say, "Baldwin Model F, key 20, string size 31," or such other description as will tell the supply house the exact position in which this particular string occurs in the scale and the key number of the note which the string completes. Instructions for sending in complete sets of bass strings for replacement will be found in supply house catalogs.

For temporary repairs when a technician breaks a bass string, there are Universal bass string replacement sets which are sold by supply houses. These include the range of bass sizes which generally will fit most pianos. Detailed instructions for using strings which you must tailor to the individual piano will be found in the catalogs.

Wire size index for single unwound piano strings

Wire Size	Diameter in inches	Wire Size	Diameter in inches
13	.031	18½	.042
13½	.032	19	.043
14	.033	19½	.044
14½	.034	20	.045
15	.035	20½	.046
15½	.036	21	.047
16	.037	21½	.048
16½	.038	22	.049
17	.039	23	.051
17½	.040	24	.055
18	.041	25	.059

Wire can be purchased in 1/4-pound, 1-pound, and even larger coils. The technician should have at least one 1/4-pound coil of each size wire in his parts inventory. Wire sizes should be closely adhered to in all pianos, for repairs as well as for complete restringing.

Tuning pins come in various sizes. For your reference, a table of sizes is given below.

Tuning pin sizes

Size	Diameter	Length in inches
1/0	.276	2-1/2, 2-3/8, 2-1/4
2/0	.281	2-1/2, 2-3/8, 2-1/4
3/0	.286	2-1/2, 2-3/8, 2-1/4
4/0	.291	2-1/2, 2-3/8, 2-1/4
5/0	.296	2-1/2, 2-3/8, 2-1/4
6/0	.301	2-3/8

As mentioned before, there are various ways to rebush loose tuning pins. On a grand, always block up under the pin block before attempting pin repairs which may loosen the layers of pin plank material. To rebush a pin, technicians may use prepared brass tuning pin bushings from supply houses and drive the pin back in. Some prefer to line the pin block hole with a strip of sandpaper and then drive or turn it in. Most tuners prefer placing a thin piece of veneer along the wall of the pin block hole and then driving the pin in to a tight fit.

The author believes it is more efficient to carry a supply of pins. Drive in a pin one size larger than the loose one. It will fit tightly without bushing.

To replace a tuning pin, remove the bent section of wire carefully from the eye. Lift the coil loosely on the pin. Turn out the old pin with a steady motion to the left. Install the new pin within the loose coils of the string. Drive in the new pin, or turn it in (driving is better because it leaves a more virgin-like surface to touch the serrations of the tuning pin within the pin block.) Replace the wire in the eye and turn the pin to the right to bring up tension. Set the coil in smooth layers around the pin. Tune two beats above pitch, lower into place, and then set the pin.

Repairing flanges

In the action, looseness may develop in the flanges which support and cooperate with the hammer butts, and in the flanges which support the damper units. To repair these units, it is necessary to carefully remove them from the action. The best way to do this is to place the action upon a flat surface so that it is well supported before you begin to remove the flanges. To remove hammer butt flanges, in certain pianos, the following procedure is recommended.

If the hammer is wobbly, and striking in such a way as to indicate that its pivot point is loose, check it by pressing the top of the jackfly to the left or right after first releasing the bridle tape from its wire mooring. With a long round-shanked screwdriver, attempt to tighten the screw which holds the hammer flange to the rail. Often this is loose, and causes the whole hammer assembly to wobble. If this screw is tight, but the butt wobbles in its flange, turn the flange screw left until only one turn remains before it falls out. Use the screw-gripping tool, or a long extension screw holder, to grip the head of the screw, turn it to the left one more turn, and remove it.

Now, remove the key that actuates that flange, if possible. This will allow the wippen to fall below its regular line and make for easy extraction of the hammer butt and flange. Ascertain if the butt and hammer can be lifted upward after setting the hammer return spring to one side. (Rest it in the groove of an adjacent hammer butt.) Either lay the adjoining hammers forward against the strings with one hand, or turn the butt being removed one quarter turn as it is being lifted, so as to clear other hammers in the action. Withdraw straight up, or once the butt is above the other butts, withdraw it first toward you, and lift it so that the hammer will clear the hammer rest rail.

Examine the flange. If the pin is loose, carefully press out the center pin using either a small center pin punch (which requires the flange to be laid on a soft wood surface and then withdrawing the pin when accessible) or a center pin extracting plier (which will not damage the bushing felt around the center pin). Replace with the next size larger center pin if the felt bushings are all right.

If the bushings are not good, but are worn oblong or otherwise defective, carefully remove the pin, cut a strip of red bushing felt about medium thick (1/4 in. in width), and taper it at one end so the point will enter the flange hole. Pull the felt through almost to the end and then place a small amount of glue around the outside edge of the remaining felt. Place the pin in the center of the collar of felt which is in the hole, with the pin absolutely straight and perpendicular to the surface of the flange, and draw the felt in until the whole inner surface of the flange hole is bushed. The pin should fit as tightly as possible but must not bind in the hole.

When the glue has set, take a sharp knife or a razor blade and trim off the felt where it protrudes from either side of the bushing hole. Don't use much glue, because it can harden the bushing and cause a rattle.

A tested method adopted by many modern technicians is to remove the flange bushing with a .099 reamer, or a drill bit of this size, held in a small tap handle or in the hammer shank reducing tool. Do the reaming as slowly as possible and do not enlarge the hole more than the diameter of the reamer. Then place a small Teflon pin bushing (called a Steinway bushing) on its inserter (both available from supply houses) and replace the pin in the bushings and eye of the hammer butt. This requires a No. 19 center pin in most cases and will allow a trouble-free repair of the flange. The author finds this the most effective method consistent with favorable conditions existing in the wooden center of the hammer butt.

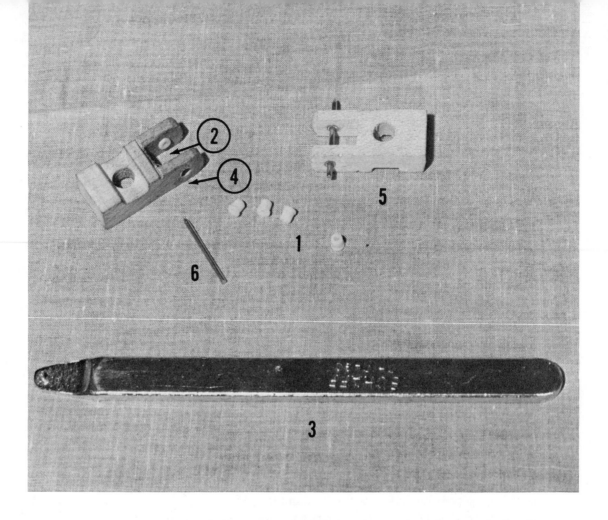

Components of flange repairs when using Teflon bushings. Small Steinway Teflon bushings (1) are installed in flange holes (2) by use of a bushing inserter (3) after the hole is reamed to .099 in. (4). This does away with rebushing old flanges (5) with felt. A No. 19 pin (6) is then installed in the Teflon bushing.

Loose pins and flange centers cause a rattle, and often result in a hard to locate "thump" when the hammer returns to rest after use. Tight center pins which have corroded, or have been tightened by humidity acting upon the wooden flange and felts, will cause sluggish hammers.

When the pin is too tight, a next size smaller pin will often fix the matter. Sometimes slight application of heat to the flange bushing will allow freedom of pin movement. Pin ease solution will clear off the corrosion, and the pin will at first seem tighter than before, but after 30 minutes or so, it will become looser. Denatured alcohol will also ease the pins. Use only a small drop on each bushing. If you hear a whistle, you usually have a corroded center pin. The bushing must be cleaned, and the pin replaced with a new center pin. Bushings can be reamed with center pins.

In all the above mentioned repairs, work carefully, and keep in mind that the tolerances are very slim indeed, since the action centers must work faster than a sewing machine and more quietly.

After repairing the flange, reinstall the hammer assembly and butt, reversing the process used for removal. Nudge the jackfly lightly to one side or the other, and, using the screw holding tool, reinsert the hammer flange screw. Tighten securely while traveling the hammer forward toward the strings to make sure you have a proper setting of the butt flange (so that the hammer will hit all three strings of its unison). Then press down on the tail of the jack, lift the wippen to its proper position (thus placing the jack under the plane of the hammer butt), and secure the bridle tape to its wire mooring. Replace the key assembly.

Corroded center balance rail pins (which come up through the center of the keys) can be cleaned with fine steel wool. Clean the front oblong-shaped key pins in a similar manner. When repairing pins in flanges, it is a good idea to think of all the pins in the action, including the key pins, and thus avoid inconsistencies in the action train from key front to hammer face.

Lesson 10 How to make special key and hammer repairs

Broken keys are repairable in a number of ways. If the break is a "green stick" break, in which the ends dovetail into each other, as is usually the case, carefully coat both broken surfaces with white glue and then rejoin. Clamp firmly with key repair clamps until dry and, if possible, place an old ivory key top on each side of the broken area as a splint. The key top can be left in place after repair, since there is usually enough clearance between adjoining keys to compensate for the extra thickness it provides.

If clearances are too small, sand the surface until enough clearance exists. Supply houses sometimes offer a broken-key repair kit which features metal splints and a doweling system to make a satisfactory repair. However, the old-ivory method has worked for hundreds of broken keys in the past. Some technicians use a thin piece of veneer instead of ivory. This is all right, and sometimes is easier to sand.

Sluggish keys (independent of the action sluggishness) are usually caused by high humidity or by something spilled into the key area of the piano. Check the key carefully and determine if it is rubbing against adjacent keys. If so, sand carefully until there is some clearance. However, if there is clearance and the key is still sluggish, investigate the front rail oblong pin. Sometimes it is turned too far and presses against the key bushing in such a way as to cause unusual friction. Adjust it until there is just a trace of side play in the key when at rest. Of course, in all cases, make sure that corrosion on the oblong pin and center rail pin is not responsible for the sluggishness. These pins can be cleaned with fine steel wool.

Occasionally, you will find that moisture and old age have caused the front key bushing felt to come loose from the inner surface of the key, or to harden to such an extent that it is unusable. There is no repair for this, short of rebushing the front of the key.

To rebush, cut a strip of bushing felt the same width as that already in the key. Place a little glue along the sides of the hole in the key front, push the felt into the hole with a key bushing wedge, and let dry. Cut a hole in the bushing so that the pin can move freely. Trim neatly to correspond to adjacent keys. The same method is used in rebushing the top center section of the key.

If the bushing is all right, the pin is clean and not turned, and yet the key sticks at the front rail, humidity has swollen the key. Use a pair of key easing pliers and squeeze the sides of the bushing until you have obtained better clearance between the bushing and the pin. Do not overdo this, since when the humidity returns to normal ranges, the keys may become too loose. In all operations such as this, be careful. If the key is too loose, turn the front rail pin slightly until proper clearances are established.

At the balance rail, you will find a complete "key button" on the top surface of the key which contains the bushing. Often the ideal repair is to install a new key button complete with bushing. Try to get the same alignment as was previously set between the top of the key and the angled edges of the new key button. There is a special key bushing tightener which resembles a square punch (as shown in the lesson on tools) which will tighten all bushings if used properly. When installing the new button, it is helpful to use two small wire brads to secure proper alignment while gluing, and to keep it right while clamping.

In some keys, small circular weights made of lead have been inserted. When you depress a key and hear a clicking sound, it will usually be due either to a loose key ivory or to a weight clicking inside the key. This will also be heard as the key is allowed to fall to rest position. However, there is also a "clacking" sound which can sometimes be heard as the jack slips back under the hammer butt. This has nothing to do with loose weights in keys. If the click is due to a loose weight, it is better to wedge the weight more securely by using a small screwdriver or punch to expand the edges against the wood of the key. Try to do this in the contour of an airplane propeller, shaped like a Y. When you are done, the key weight surface should show the marks at its edges 120° apart.

If you hear a clack instead of a click when the key is released, just as the jack snaps back under the hammer butt, examine the lower front surface of the hammer butt. Usually you will find that the felt pad which is glued to this area is gone, either due to moth damage or its having fallen from where it was originally glued. If this is the case, glue a new hammer butt square felt to the area so that the jack top will not cause noise when the jack spring pushes it into its normal at-rest position.

Hammer shanks

Hammer heads must be glued securely to hammer stems. Otherwise there will be wobbly hammer heads, or deterioration of tone, or both. To reglue a hammer stem, clean out the hole in the head and clean the surface of the stem. Place glue on the stem in such a way that you can "twirl" the head onto it, leaving a small collar of glue surrounding the place where the stem enters the head.

If the hammer stem or shank is broken, you can replace it with a new shank, after slowly boring out the old hole in the hammer butt and in the hammer head. Do not enlarge the holes. Do not change the angle at which the head is fastened to the shank. Reglue, and while the glue is drying, travel the hammer to the unison, making sure that the head strikes all three strings evenly and as close to the original striking point as you can possibly make it.

To fix a broken shank without replacing it, apply glue to both broken surfaces, wrap with strong thread while drying, and leave the thread in place after the glue is dry. Supply houses sell tubular hammer shank repair splints made of metal. These are used by some technicians for quick repairs. Make sure, if you use these, that there will be no loosening of the tubular splint after the glue has dried on the shank. It is my judgment that this repair can easily change the tone of the note being played by a particular hammer, and in fact, all glue repairs to hammer shanks can result in significant tone change in a unison. For that reason the best "repair" is replacement of the broken shank with a new one.

When installing replacement shanks, use shanks of the same wood as the worn shanks. If replacing maple, use maple. If repairing a fine piano which has cedar shanks in the treble (and in some older quality pianos, throughout the piano scale), use cedar shanks for replacements. Always remember your days playing baseball and align the grain of the hammer shank so that it is held in the same position as the baseball bat was (with the trademark up). There is no trademark on a hammer shank, but the grain is visible, and putting the grain in a different relationship with the hammer head striking point will change the tone of that unison. Pretend the hammer felt portion is the baseball, and the shank is the bat.

There is a tool on the market which will remove hammer heads as the screw is tightened in the handle of the tool, after the glue has been heated. It is the safest and quickest method of removing a hammer head from a shank.

If the back check is loose on the wire at the end of a grand piano key, the same clicking sound will be heard as when a weight is loose. Hours of searching may be saved if one remembers this simple fact. To repair, run the back check down one more turn on the wire, or if necessary, apply pin block restorer (one drop) at the point where the wire enters the back check. Sluggish hammer return can be due to weak hammer return springs in upright actions. Increase the normal curvature of the spring, or install a repair replacement.

Squeaks which occur in the action are often due to insufficient lubrication where the damper return springs contact the damper levers. Do not use oil. Only flake graphite or a mixture of petroleum jelly and graphite will do. Whenever possible, use Ivory soap. It is cleaner and usually better.

In some actions the hammer butt flanges are fastened to a brass rail. To repair these units, action removal is required. Using a long, thin screwdriver, you can tighten the flange screws. However, the metal in old brass rail actions is usually crystallized and the flange units are easily broken. Replacement flange clips, butt plates, and flanges are carried by supply houses.

Bridle tape replacements come in various types. The clip-on type makes a quick, secure repair. Cut off the old bridle tape as closely as possible to the hammer butt, fasten the clip to the protruding stem, thread it through the hole (if any), and secure it to the bridle wire. Adjust so that there is no slack when the soft pedal is fully depressed, but loose enough that the key corresponding to the note is not moved when the pedal is pushed down. Cork-tip tapes may also be used. Simply insert them in the holes of the back catch and adjust.

Split tapes, which have one end split to allow them to be slipped over the back catch, will interfere with other back catches if not carefully drawn tight. Regular bridle tapes can be tacked in place with the installing tools sold by suppliers, or fastened in place with one drop of hot glue. For this purpose, the hot melt glue gun, which uses round sticks of glue, is handy. This unit, made by United Shoe Machinery, is convenient and has many applications in piano work.

Keys and their coverings

Ivory keys become yellow because they are not exposed to light. You can make them a little whiter by using fine sandpaper or ivory polish obtainable from supply houses. Mix ivory white with denatured alcohol and rub or buff electrically. It is preferable to use ivory wafers when regluing ivory to a key, since the application of heat and moisture causes the wafer under the key top to make a fine bond to the key, and the area which might show through the ivory is white. Use glue which will show up white when regluing ivories, even if you have to mix oxide of zinc (from an art supply store) with the glue. Ivory cement is already white.

Save your old ivories. They are becoming more expensive, and sometimes will make a better match on a keyboard you are repairing than new ivories. The application of heat will loosen the cement holding old ivories to keys, and they can be removed easily with just a slight tug upwards and away from the key.

Modern pianos for the most part use ivorine, which is a name given to various white plastic covering substances. This can be bought in sheets, in ready-cut key blanks, and in various thicknesses. If you send your complete keyboard to the supply house for recovering, you have no worries on this matter, but if you should want to recover a keyboard yourself, the following ideas are advanced from the author's experience.

1. Use the thickest ivorine you can afford. The lighter the stock, the more ripples are possible, the more likely the glue will warp the stock, and the less mirrorlike your key surfaces will be.

2. If you should purchase a complete key-recovering sytem, which costs hundreds of dollars, further instructions are unnecessary. If you do not purchase such a unit, read on.

3. After carefully removing old key coverings, gauge the thickness of the material you will use to recover the keys, and set a small planer or table saw with a fine blade so that it will remove an amount from the upper surface of the key wood that exactly corresponds to the thinness or thickness of your new covering material.

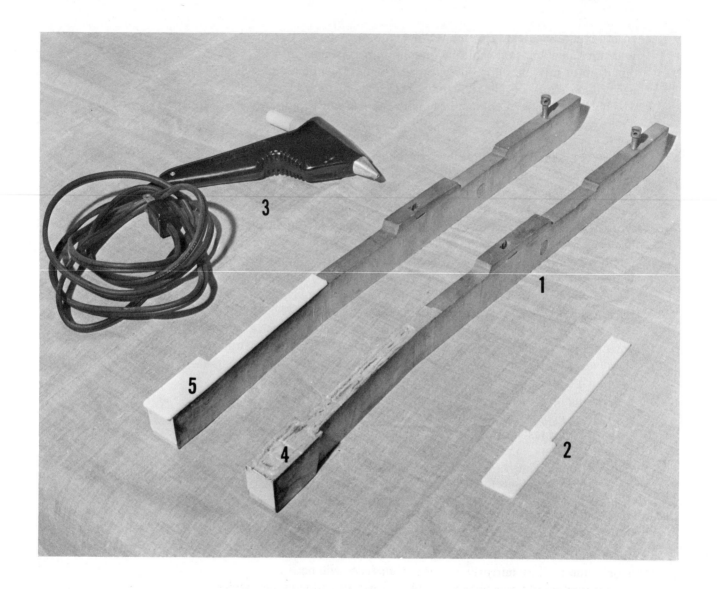

Re-covering old keys may be done in the following way: Remove the old ivory from the key (1), and level the key surface to receive the new covering, an Apsco key top (2), which is molded to fit each note of the scale. A Thermogrip glue gun (3) with 60-second bonding glue is used to cement tops to keys. Glue bead is applied (4) immediately prior to pressing on the new top covering. The new key top is installed on the old key (5).

4. Run the keys through the planer or saw set-up, removing a fine layer of wood in the proper dimensions from the flat upper surfaces of the keys. Make certain that the top surface remains absolutely perpendicular to the sides of the keys! Continue the cut to a spot 1/2 in. to the rear of the place where the old key coverings ended.

5. Using ivorine cement, place the new key blanks on the keys, clamping each one with a key clamp until the glue has dried. (It is useful at this point to have a definite measurement for the ''lip'' or overhang you desire at the front of the key.) Or, using the ready molded key tops from Apsco, do all the Cs, then the Ds, and so on, until all keys are covered. Ivorine cement in this method is not essential, since contact cement will work just as well or better.

The author uses a Thermogrip glue gun, running a clear bead of hot glue 1/8 in. from the outer surface of the keys and pressing down firmly with the complete hand for 30 seconds on each newly installed key top. When installed in this way, any attempt to remove the key top without the application of heat will result in removal of a layer of wood under the key top. This is a sound, solid method of application. It is also rapid, since there is no need to clamp the keys and wait for glue to set. Using the heavy, ready-molded key tops eliminates ripples and waves in the finished product.

6. Carefully hand-file the edges that protrude along the sides of the keys with a fine ivorine file. Finish the edges with fine garnet paper.

7. If, by chance, you should damage the top finish on thick ivorine plastic, imperfections can be removed by buffing with an electric buffing wheel which is liberally charged with Tripoli ivory polish. Even deep gouges, intentionally created with a pocket knife, can be removed in this way and the surface can be made mirror-like. Do not overheat the plastic with the running wheel.

8. Replace the keys in the piano. The removal of the exact thickness of the new covering material allows the thickness of the old covering to make up for the application of glue. Thus, when finished, the keys have pretty much the same height alignment in the piano as the original keyboard. This saves a lot of work with punchings and capstans.

Recoat damaged sharps with black lacquer. If the damage is too extensive to be repaired by this treatment, replace with new sharps.

Repair of sharps

Lesson 11 How to make a piano that will sell

Once you have a piano, either old or not so old, that has received proper regulation, has had the key level laid (perhaps with new key tops installed), has had all hammers traveled correctly and the various strings and bridges made right, you have, through your work, an instrument of considerable added value. Still, it may not have a smooth, even transition of tone from one section to the next, or even from one note to the next. It is time to look at the possible reshaping and voicing of the hammers in order to arrive at a mellifluous sound which will sell the piano.

Not only shop-treated pianos, but others, require this treatment. The company with the finest reputation in the business advises customers to have their pianos regulated periodically, and to have the tone quality smoothed out every two or three years under normal use. This is an operation which must be performed skillfully and requires considerable practice both of ear and hand before you will get really good at it. For that reason, it is better to shape hammers and voice them in your shop on your own instrument before going into homes and auditoriums to attempt such critical work.

Reshaping of hammers is done both manually and with the aid of electric sanding tools. Most oldline technicians prefer to do the job manually, using a sandpaper file or board, and reconstructing the hammer outline completely by hand. This is the most precise way to do it. A piano which is perfectly tuned may still sound bad, because of the harmonics which are being produced. A string will sound much differently when played by a hard hammer than when played by a soft one. In addition, over years of use, some striking surfaces of the hammers become deeply ridged by the string cuts which constantly are occurring. Often, the complete striking surface of the hammer will become flat and hard, losing the rounded, smooth surface of its original design.

Reshaping hammers

Reshaping is often the best single cure for harsh or ''plucking'' tones which originate when the string sinks deeply into the hammer grooves and is almost plucked as the hammer hits it. Hard hammers cause higher harmonics to resound more strongly, and soft hammers (too soft) give a mushy tone. Ideally, the hammer should be in such condition that its stroke upon the string sets the string vibrating throughout its length with fundamentals, second harmonics, and third harmonics the stronger. A piece of sandpaper tacked to a strip of wood about 1/2 in. wide will suffice for single hammers. In gang-filing hammers, a wider sandpaper board must be used.

Remove the action from the piano and place it on the bench with the hammer rail resting securely on some surface. Begin at the hammer molding, where the felt just begins to swell, and stroke the file toward the head of the hammer. Follow the contour of the hammer head with strokes evenly divided between its bottom and top surfaces. When each stroke arrives at the crown of the hammer, dress it during the completion of your stroke so that a slight curl of felt is created at this point, projecting away from the crown.

Do not file across this striking surface. What you are trying to do is to slowly remove the top layer of felt, not at the crown of the hammer, but from the shoulder beginning all the way to the crown. This is because the crown area has already had the top layer cut through and destroyed in most cases by the strings. Consider the layers of felt on a hammer to be like the layers of an onion. To get a better picture of this, cut an onion in half, then slice it. Picture the hammer wood molding as inserted into the side of the slice of onion and reaching to the exact center. Now you have a composite picture of a hammer, that might serve you as an aid in reshaping hammers. After both bottom and top of the hammer have been dressed in this way, lightly brush across the crown (or striking surface) to remove the felt curl. Avoid filing into the frontal surface of the hammer.

Always retain the pearlike shape of the hammer from shoulder around the crown to shoulder. Do not remove more felt than is absolutely necessary to regain the shape of the hammer. In gang-filing, especially as practiced on grand action hammers, three or even four hammers may be held firmly by one hand and all filed at the same time to the same contour. The complete process is exactly the same, however. If you wish, a light pass with fine garnet paper across the crown area will finish the job. Do not use coarse sandpaper as it combs the felt. The author has found the metallic fine sandpaper, as shown in the lesson on tools, to be especially useful in hammer filing, since it can be shaped to fit the hand and the contours desired in the hammer. But the method is always the same.

Some craftsmen use a Moto-tool, or a similar electric, drum-sanding hand tool to reshape hammers. This is satisfactory for quick work on pianos that are in terrible shape. But for fine work on the best pianos, the most trustworthy method is still the hand-filing method. However, if you desire to cut the time involved by using an electric tool, I suggest that you also buy a speed reducing control for it. It is not the electric tool that gouges hammers. It is the technician who cannot control it lightly enough to remove only the top layer of felt with each pass over the hammer. Cutting the speed down and using the finest possible sanding drumhead makes this unit controllable, and some men do fine work with it.

Never use sharp instruments when you work on hammers. Do not file across any portion of the hammer. When in doubt as to being able to improve the shape of the hammers, don't file at all. It is a privilege to watch an accomplished technician file hammers. He uses the file with simple, graceful motions. Cultivate this work habit when touching a file to a hammer. You are not filing wood, but relatively soft layers of felt of very high quality.

Treble hammers

Sometimes it is obvious that the treble hammers do not require as much filing on their already thin and compressed surfaces. They are more likely to need repair of the striking surface. Some technicians glue thin strips of buckskin on the complete flat surfaces of the hammers at this point, in an attempt to reconstitute the striking surface. Wherever possible, replace the complete hammer. But when this is impossible, buckskin will present an acceptable striking surface. Keep all glue from the striking surface, and from either side of the skin. Such attempted repairs of the treble striking surfaces are second-best, and their success will depend on the quality of the material used. Self-adhesive moleskin and the like will cover the hammers but the results will not be up to high standards.

Construction of the hammer

Some knowledge of construction will help in your attempts at reshaping and resurfacing. At the factory, the hammer molding board (which is not yet cut to assume identity as individual hammer moldings, but is tapered in its length to contain all the hammer moldings for a complete set) is set above a caul. The caul, which is steamed or otherwise heated, is then lined with a strip of hammer felt which may be 3-1/2 to 4 in. wide at its widest point. It will be much thicker in the middle throughout its length than the thickest hammer encountered in the piano. Under pressure, the molding board is inserted, with its surfaces coated with glue, into the felt hammer strip.

As the pressure increases, the hammer felt is compressed around the more pointed edge of the molding board, and at complete inserting, is traveled back up onto the shoulder of the molding. At this point, where the felt is secured to the shoulder, a wire staple is often placed. It prevents slippage in pressure of the compressed felt which now surrounds the molding board.

Then the molding board is sawed into the individual hammers, graduated in size throughout according to both the contours of the moldings and the relative thickness of the hammer felt strip. Obviously, the point of separation at each edge of the hammer will swell outward and present a higher outline when one looks straight across the flat striking surface of the hammer than will the middle of the flat section, since pressure is not so easily released in that section. Therefore, it is customary in well-made pianos for some hammer shaping to be done before the piano is put on the market. However, in pianos which are mass-produced without this significant detail, you will find uneven tone because the striking surface of the new hammer is not hitting all strings in the unison at precisely the same time.

The same thing holds true when you replace an old hammer with a new one. The striking surface should be dressed delicately so that the surface contacts all strings in the unison equally and at the exact same time. The shape of the hammer has a bearing on the tone of a piano. New or old, pianos require proper hammer care and shaping if they are to function as they should.

Voicing hammers

One could write a book on voicing hammers and all the theories and working methods that are available. For our purposes, we shall discuss methods which have been tried and found to improve piano tone, and avoid those which might lead to disaster if not completely understood.

Voicing may become a muscular exercise, since compressed felt strongly resists penetration by needles. However, voicing pliers are available for those who want them, and can be set for various depths of penetration. In this matter of voicing, as in all piano craftsmanship, it is better to "measure two times before sawing once." Therefore, I suggest you adhere to manual voicing without the use of pliers until you are certain your work *improves* the tone when you do use pliers. Ruin your own piano while practicing, if you wish, but never a client's.

Begin at the lower bass end of the piano and thrust the voicing needle into the hammer at a point where the shoulder just begins to swell. (This will usually be at the point above the forward tip of the molding.) The depth of penetration should be not more than two-thirds of the thickness of the felt from molding to shoulder.

Try sticking the under side of the hammer in precisely the same place and the same way. *Do not come in from the side and separate the felt layers.* Always work from the flat top and bottom surfaces of the hammer. Try the tone. If nothing much has happened, thrust the *single* voicing needle again into the hammer on top and bottom at a point 1/16 in. toward the crown from the first penetration. Try the tone. You now have four stitches in the hammer (two on top, two on bottom).

If it is necessary to soften more, proceed moving in small increments of 1/16 in. toward the crown, always duplicating the stitches on the top with stitches on the bottom, until you reach a point 1/16 in. from the striking point area. *Do not penetrate the striking surface of the hammer!*

If this work is not enough, shorten your penetration to one-third of the thickness of hammer and stitch in a zigzag pattern in the same areas as before. Try the tone after each pass with the voicing needle! More pianos are ruined by over-softening the hammer than by having

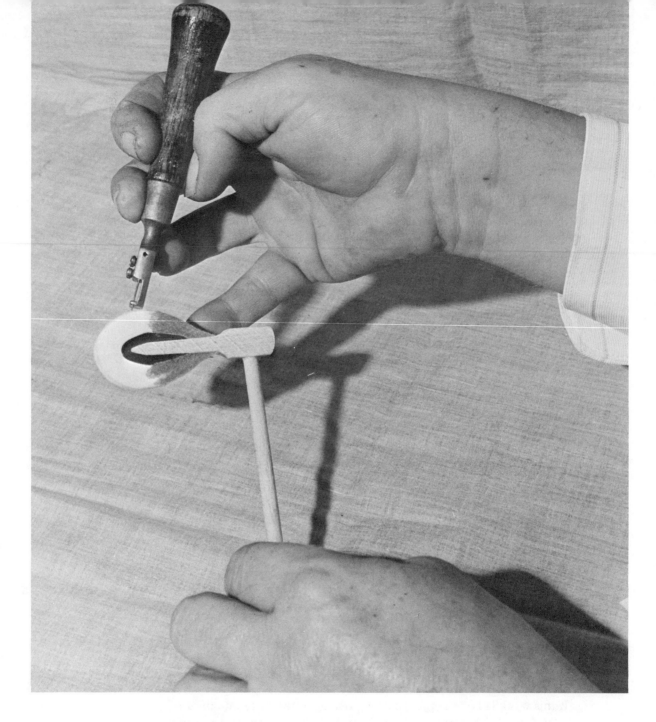

The beginning stitch in hammer voicing is made on the top of the hammer. Subsequent stitches continue around the shoulders of the hammer. Do not penetrate the striking point area.

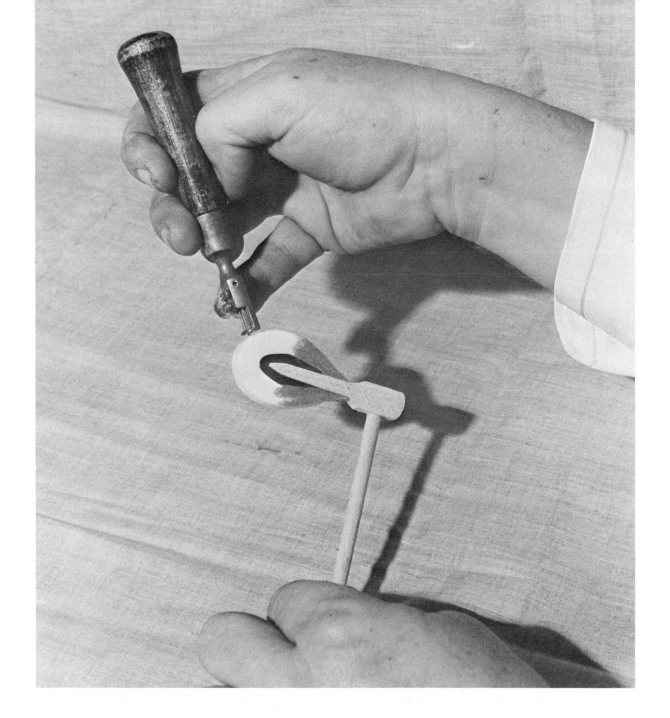

The second top stitch is made nearer the crown of the hammer. Each stitch is duplicated on the bottom, or opposite side, of the hammer. Again, the actual striking area is not penetrated.

it too hard. *When in doubt, leave the hammer hard.* Usually, the lower bass end requires no more than four stitches in the first octave. The next octave usually requires three stitches; the next two octaves, two stitches; and the next two octaves, one stitch. But you cannot work in quantity. You must work with each individual hammer and get its tone to match the one just completed before going on to another hammer.

Supply houses sell a smoothing iron to harden the surface of the hammers when they are too soft. Heat it, and iron the felt. Also, some lacquer preparations are sold for hardening hammers, but you have no control over these preparations.

When you are done voicing, all tones should blend gradually as you go up the scale, with both a firm and light playing touch. The goal of skilled voicing is to provide a tone that has no great discrepancy between loud and soft playing of the piano. Your ear must accustom itself to the nuances of tone which may be produced by a hammer before you will be able to voice satisfactorily. But you might as well try it, since the only way your ear can become accustomed to proper tone is to have your hands produce it and then alter it, and in the process, recognize it.

This is basic voicing, and such other methods as men may devise are usually a matter of personal opinion and, like most things, when done well, work well. You will improve your method with little niceties as you continue to practice voicing, and that is as it should be. However, before adding anything to this method, whether you are experienced or a novice, try following the simple progression and see if it won't solve most voicing requirements.

Adjusting the touch   When you encounter a sticky or sluggish action which seems to be harder to play than the pianist would desire, check first to make sure you have free traveling keys on their center rail pins and without undue friction in the front bushings. Once this is certain, lubricate the bushings with a light touch of graphite. Shine the top of the capstan screws until there is no roughness present, and lubricate the felt, upon which the capstan thrust is received, with soap or graphite. (Some use a spray Teflon lube for this and the following items; the author uses a concoction of his own manufacture.) Lubricate all top ends of the jacks, the damper lever spring slot, and the hammer return spring slots.

Make sure the spoon of the dampers does not contact the end of the damper lever until the hammer has traveled halfway to the string. The pressure of 60 to 70 damper springs added to the total pressure friction in the action makes a great resistance in the action. Check the jack and adjust the capstans so that the jack begins to lift the hammer butt just momentarily after the key is beginning to come down under your finger. In other words, establish just a suspicion of lost motion between the beginning of a key stroke and the lift of the hammer butt.

Often you will find that the felt pads upon which the hammer rail rests have become dented, and the hammer travel is just a fraction too long from rest position to string. When this is true, you can lift the hammer rail slightly and shim under the felts so that the hammer travel is correct, thus lifting the butts slightly off the tops of the jacks and making a rapid repeating action. There must always be clearance enough for the jacks to slip back under the butts when the key is released slowly. Check this especially in damp weather when the action parts have grown slightly.

Once in a while you will find that someone wants the touch made heavier. To do this, you can strengthen or increase the pressure of the damper springs, and allow the dampers to start to lift at the moment the key is depressed. Also, strengthen the hammer springs. If even more resistance is desired, additional weight can be placed upon the back section of the keys by adding Jiffy key weights, which fasten on easily. Space them along each key so that all keys seem to have the same resistance to touch. It is better to leave key weighting to the factory, since the overall ratio of action performance is affected by what you do here. But it can be done, when necessary.

Restyling the case on old uprights

A glance at most old pianos reveals that they were built to appear larger and stronger than they are. The legs are large, bulky blocks which also contain the front casters. The upper front is massive and so designed that the top protrudes outward to make the piano seem almost top-heavy. In addition, the top is massive, as though it were designed to sustain the weight of the pianist. Much of this case design was quite in style in the past, but it is garish in modern surroundings. A fine piano may look like an ugly, old giant. There are ways to make these monsters appear more modern and thus more inviting to those who seek an inexpensive piano for a child to learn on.

An upright is laid back on a cart. Saw cuts on the sides of the piano have been completed, creating a new configuration of the sides and top.

For many years, the author has been restyling pianos and he knows of many others who do the same. While you may have aesthetic inclinations which are in contrast to mine, it might be useful to know what methods can be used to make a salable unit of an old upright.

One of the simplest ways to restyle an old piano is to lay it on its back, remove the front casters, and relocate the holes for these as close to the front of the case as possible, while still retaining the lower wooden girder blocks. Then cut off the lower projecting blocks squarely, coat the front area thus exposed with contact cement, and cement new veneer on this square bald end. Spray the new veneer with a sealer at this time. Use a rubber hammer to install the veneer, pounding it down firmly and hand-filing the edges to a taper after the glue has set.

Remove the legs which are fastened to the bottom of the key bed, and save them for possible future use. If you like, modern legs are available (from supply houses) which have a caster (small) or ball end. They will reach from key bed to floor, and give a more modern appearance to the piano. The old legs can be made into lovely candlesticks, and often into beautiful lamps.

Stand the piano upon its casters and remove the piano hinge or the strap hinges which lock the front of the top in place. Remove the top board completely and set it aside. You will be using it later. Remove everything which rests upon the top of the piano, thus exposing the upper edge of the pin block and back. Using 1/8-in. plywood or masonite, make a cover for the exposed pin block and top of the back which will project 1/2 in. forward past the point of the outer edges of the longest tuning pins in the piano. Cement this top in place, tapering the edges by hand.

Measure the highest point at which the action juts upward toward the top of the piano. Now mark the side of the piano so that you can make a downward saw cut at precisely the point where your newly installed top piece contacts the side. Cut down to a point 1 in. above the highest point of the action. Make this saw cut with precision, and exactly vertical to the bottom of the case.

Remove the front music supporting board, after marking the place where a horizontal line drawn from the bottom of your recent cut would intersect the side of the ''gingerbread'' installed on the upper front of the piano. Proceed to cut horizontally, from the upper front of the case to the end of the cut you recently made, and remove the block of wood cut out of each side of the piano.

Measure the amount of projection which you will encounter in replacing the front music rack system (which you will now cut down to the dimensions of the new top height of the piano). Using the old top of the piano, preferably the front section, saw off enough of the rearward portion to permit the old top to be installed clear back to the vertical cut on each side, and with enough overhang in front to encompass the most forward measurement of the music rack. Cut down to size, and replace the old music rack front, using the same retaining system that held it in the old, larger case, but relocating the various catches to hold the new front.

Drill a hole through the top on each end, about 2 in. from its front edge, so that a screw placed through it will encounter either the side board of the piano case, or the tops of the pedestals which stand on either side of the old music rack system. Countersink two wood screws in these holes, with the tops of the screws just level with the surface of the top.

Measure the area now left exposed on top of the piano front. This measurement, from side to side, and from the upper surface of the old top to the lower surface of the new, thin top sheet, is the size of a plate glass mirror to order for this piano. Have the glass people place a hole clear through the mirror at a point exactly halfway down from the top on each edge, and in 1 in. from the outer edges. Less than this distance in and the mirror will crack.

Using a vacuum cleaner, remove the sawdust you have dropped into the piano parts. Next remove the action and keys.

Carefully remove all hinges at the fall board, all rubber topped nails, and all knobs from the piano. Re-cover the keys.

At this point, you have considerable work to do. First you must decide, depending on the piano case finish condition, if you intend to revarnish the piano (after stripping it of all old varnish). Sometimes, a simple application of check eradicating varnish will suffice. Or you may decide to refinish using the lacquer method. Whatever way you choose will require that you begin filling in the dents and scratches on the case with a lacquer or shellac stick. And, of course, where large areas of old veneer have become loosened, you will want to re-cement them with veneer cement. All edges will have to be stained. The final result of any finish will depend almost 80% upon the smoothness of your work as you prepare the wood for refinishing. Preparing the case for the finish is the most important part of this process.

To remodel this old upright, the top, sides, and front were altered. The old music desk was removed, shortened, and reinstalled using the original mountings, pivots and catches. A mirror will be installed to cover the exposed section of top pins. Parts: 1) music rack or desk; 2) music shelf; 3) sharp or black keys; 4) natural or white keys; 5) key slip; 6) sustain pedal; 7) sostenuto pedal; 8) soft pedal; 9) bottom front board.

This piano has been refinished in pecan spatter, and has new key coverings, basic brass fittings from a decorator's store, and new brass knobs. The center escutcheon on the music rack is plastic sprayed with gold lacquer and then given two coats of clear lacquer. The mirror at the top has not yet been installed, nor has the name decal been affixed at the center of the fall board.

As an aid in inspiration, study the illustrations of a cut-down and refinished piano recently completed in the author's shop. Much of what would take thousands of words to explain can be seen at a glance.

On older grand pianos, you will often find double legs, and on very old models, massive round, and lavishly fluted ones. Most grands are designed to make the total picture of legs and case a pleasing one. However, if a client should desire a more contemporary design, you

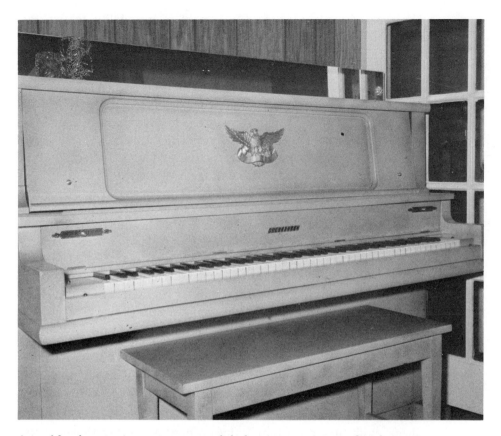

An old player piano was remodeled, given a pecan finish, and a mirror to give the effect shown. Notice how the mirror creates an illusion of a smaller piano. The player doors on the top section were removed and a light plywood insert was placed behind the counter area. The original music rack hinges were retained, and the old top was altered to fit the new style.

can buy modern single legs and installation plates from the supply houses. The same holds true for the pedal lyre system.

Music desks of a more recent design are also available for grands and can do much to change the style, since the case is usually almost the same as the most modern piano. Therefore, you can make a new-looking grand out of an old-looking grand with somewhat less trouble than is required for restyling uprights. The selling price is, of course, much higher.

The care of a piano case is important. Your ability to use the proper polish and lemon oil will be amply rewarded in the fine appearance of pianos which you recondition. Buy a scratch remover kit from a supply house and some sticks of wood edge stain to touch up those pianos you tune and overhaul. Use the amalgamator and check eradicating fluids as shown in the catalogs, and you will be able to recondition the finish on some old pianos which appear to require complete removal of the old varnish. Varnish can be sprayed or brushed over old lacquer surfaces. But lacquer will dissolve, and during the process of curing, will damage a varnished finish.

Restoring the finish

One of the dependable ways to remove checked places in old varnish is to use pumice stone and an oblong piece of wood about 5 in. long by 2 in. thick and about 4 in. wide, on the wider surface of which a firm piece of felt has been affixed. Dip the block and felt in plenty of water and rub across the checks with the powdered pumice stone. Scrub well and use water generously. (Lava soap has a considerable pumice content and may sometimes be used.) Clean off the pumice deposits on the finish and rub with the same wet block and pumice stone. Then polish the wood with the palm of the hand, using a fine grade of furniture polish. Finally, rub well with a lint-free cheesecloth. Moisten the cloth with wood alcohol and rub to bring out the gloss.

Check eradicator dries rapidly into a hard and shiny finish. If the finish is too shiny, dull it by careful polishing with extra fine steel wool and, where necessary, gasoline. You can, after applying eradicator, apply Constantines Wonder Glo or a fine varnish, very watery in consistency, right over the eradicator. This does a rather good job in many cases.

When you encounter an abrasion on a piano case, as where some hard object has dented the surface, you can carefully moisten the area with hot water and cover it with some thicknesses of unprinted paper. Then, by means of a hot iron or other heat producing surface applied over the moist area, you can raise the wood fibers up to the surface level again. This, of course, will make some changes in the varnish in that area, but by using techniques already described, you can restore the varnish to an acceptable appearance.

Burning-in operations with lacquer and stick shellacs are not easily done unless you practice for quite some time on discarded pieces of piano cases. But if you will get a burn-in knife, some stick shellac, and practice using them, you will find that this method will fill dents as no other method will.

In the case of old pianos which have been heavily decorated, often with artfully carved scrolls and figures, it is helpful to step back a pace or two and consider if the beauty of the piano may not be better revealed by antiquing. For this purpose, the many antiquing kits now on the market offer a wide variety of finishes and decorative effects.

Antiquing

One of the author's clients began his ownership of pianos with an old, ornate, tall one which was lavishly decorated with scrolls. The author antiqued it fire engine red, and then shaded it, according to the instructions on the kit, with streaks of brown rubbing ink in the direction of graining. Then the scroll work was decorated with gold rubbing wax which when hardened could be buffed to a high shine. An old four-legged, claw-footed wind-up stool was located, finished the same way, and installed with the piano.

Sometimes it is preferable not to cut an old piano. If in your eyes the case has character, and with antiquing you can bring out the beauty, you can make an old, ornate piano valuable. In this case, also, remember that the preparation of the surface is more important than the actual painting. Follow the directions on the antiquing kit and all should turn out well. A good trick when applying gold to decorative areas is to mix a little of the base coat (red, or whatever it is) with the gold. Then the gold does not stand out like new paint but seems to be more in harmony with the antique finish of the piano.

In closing this lesson, let us encompass a few facts that make all this work worthwhile. People who are looking for older pianos are hoping to find good, resonant tone, like that which they remember in the old parlor upright at Grandma's house. You can give it to them with careful action reconditioning and regulation, plus attention to the repairs and first aid methods (advanced in this book) for bass strings and other components. They are also looking for something they won't have to apologize for when their friends see it. By restyling, you can often place these old pianos in lavish homes. The author has done this often.

By playing down the colors, you can refinish or antique in a moderate and subdued way so that the instrument will not seem freshly painted. With all dents and scratches removed, new key tops and beautiful black sharps, a piano looks good. Many people are looking for a piano that the kids can learn to play on, and they intend to trade up to a finer instrument in the future. You will find, if you do your work well, that they will come to you for consultation when it is time to buy a finer instrument.

From upright to console to grand is the pattern for those who learn to love the unique mystery of the piano. You can begin their pilgrimage to musical beauty by making them the owners of a fine reconditioned upright. Then you will have another tuning customer, too. In addition, you will probably be the one who sells them the console, or influences their decision to buy a fine quality instrument from your dealer friend. And finally, you will be the one who is the trusted professional to whom they turn when the epitome of the piano, the grand, needs competent care.

But, in the beginning, people will be looking at the piano as just another piece of furniture. Try to keep that in mind, and don't judge them too harshly. After all, someday they may become your good friends and thanks to you, have a grand in their living room.

Just a few hints on restyling: Before cutting across the front or down the sides, try to style the piano so that the mirror will occupy two-fifths of the total space above the flat music shelf above the keys. There is no hard and fast rule on this, but the design is better if you keep within these proportions. On old players, instead of trying to redo the sliding door at the bottom and leaving a hole to cover, just cover the complete bottom front with thin masonite or very thin 1/8-in. plywood; then spray. Sometimes it is easier to cover the front area on the top of an old player, too.

Of course, it goes without saying that you replace the hinges and their key ways after polishing them. New brass knobs look best. New rubber-tipped nails should be used in place of those removed.

If the side of the case is too thick to make the necessary holes for holding your mirror, cut a small piece of wood for each side, glue with aliphatic glue to the inside of the case where you want the screws to go, and clamp until well set. Use rosettes and decorative mirror-holding screws for installing the mirror. Often it is a good idea to place a large piece of foam rubber just above the center section of the tuning pins. Then, if the lady of the house decides to clean the mirror, she won't bend its center back against the tuning pins and break it. Also, light, flat pieces of felt glued to the case at the point where the mirror sides make contact will help prevent mirror damage.

Lesson 12 Restringing grand pianos

Restringing of grand pianos is usually done by people who have had training in a factory, or by enterprising technicians who sought out the experts and learned from them. Certainly, one of the better ways to learn this part of the piano maker's craft is to get an old grand and pay a craftsman who is experienced in this field to assist you in mastering the complete operation. Even with the information provided in this lesson, supplemented by the extensive material presented in this text, one should not string a grand and set dampers without some professional supervision. By all means, locate a reputable craftsman who is actively engaged in rebuilding grands and be guided by his methods.

To make it possible for the student to approach the subject of stringing grands, an art form in itself, the following procedures are supplied. They work better if performed in the sequence in which they are given. As in all piano work, they work better, too, if the technician is actively thinking about what he is doing.

Remove the top, top hinges, music desk, and all accouterments along the sides of the grand which might interfere with removal later of the cast iron plate. Draw a small sketch of the top surface of the grand. Measure from the side of the case to the plate. Record this measurement on the sketch at a point corresponding with its location on the piano. Measure on the left front side twice, and record. Make similar measurements on the right front side and record these also.

Now mark the center of the longest part of the plate, at the rear of the grand, and make a corresponding mark on the wood of the inner case just opposite the mark on the plate. (The plate must be installed in precisely the same position in which you found it. These measurements and marks are very important for all pianos and will align the plate just as it was before you began your work.)

Place stiff cardboard or small sheets of veneer as a protective covering around the inner sides of the case. Affix them with masking tape or some other fastener. You must protect the inner surfaces of the case sides because they can be easily scraped as you remove the 400 to 500 pound harp. Also cover the top edges of the case. Leave no areas uncovered.

Calculating down bearing and letting down tension

Now use a down bearing gauge to gauge the amount of bearing in the lower bass, middle bass, upper bass, lower tenor, upper tenor, lower treble, middle treble, and upper treble. If there is insufficient down bearing at any of these points, mark the areas of weakness on your sketch and, by some significant mark, on the bridges concerned. You will have to increase this down bearing while rebuilding the piano. If insufficient down bearing exists throughout the piano, you will have to make a choice as to whether to move the harp when you reinstall it to a position slightly lower than it was originally, or to shim up the bridges, either with new, thicker bridge caps or by restoring the crown to the sound board (if that is the cause of lowered bearing). Record the down bearing measurements on your sketch of the bridges.

Remove all braided cotton which has been interwoven in the hitch pin ends of the strings.

Beginning at the lower bass, let down the tension on one outside string per unison from bottom bass to top treble in the piano. Then let down the tension of the other outside string on each unison. Finally, let down the tension of the middle string of each unison. Do not vary this procedure, since you may cause severe damage to the harp if you do. You have now released the tension evenly throughout the entire piano.

Removing the dampers

Remove the fall board and its accouterments. Remove the action from the piano. Beginning at the bottom bass, loosen the damper wire-holding screws on each damper wire, from inside the key bed area. The author has seen cases where the technician or some dealer with a great deal of nerve has attempted to restring a grand without removing the dampers. The result will be broken and misaligned dampers and the restringing job will be four times as hard to do if the dampers are left in the piano.

Using either an old pin block, with holes already drilled, or a long board, make a series of holes in a line so that you will be able to keep the dampers in proper order as they came out of the piano. Lift each damper out carefully and place in your newly-made damper rack, in the exact order in which the dampers were removed from the piano. Avoid bending any part of the damper assembly while doing this operation.

Removing the strings

Using a string gauge or micrometer, begin at the first string at the right top treble and carefully gauge the wire size used for that unison. Write this down. Then proceed unison by unison downward to the bass, measuring each unison and marking down the transitions of string size noted. Mark on the sketch of the grand plate any loops which terminate single strings.

Now using music wire cutters, cut one outside string of each unison as closely to the tuning pin as possible; or, better yet, using the coil punch, which should have a hollowed center long enough to go down over the pin and the coil, tap hard enough to cut the wire at the pin eye, and cut one outside unison string in each unison. Go back to the bass after this and cut the other outside string loose from the pin. Then cut the center strings loose. Remove all strings from the tenor and treble and discard them.

String the bass strings on a copper wire so that they remain in proper order from top to bottom; use a punching along the wire to take the place of any bass string which is missing. Coil these in a long group, box them and after enclosing the model and serial numbers of the piano, send them off to be duplicated.

Checking the pin block and tuning pins

Make sure that the pin is in approximately the position it would be above the plate if the string were still on it. Test the grip between the pins and the pin block. If the grip or friction between pin block hole and tuning pin is less than 175 pounds per inch as tested with a torque wrench, you will have to consider whether to use the next size larger pin in restringing or to replace the pin block.

The author favors discarding the old pin block and replacing with a new one if the friction is too light, because any structural weakness in an old pin block will not be solved by driving in larger tuning pins. Furthermore, the block will not get tighter since it is usually the lack of tuning consistency which has made restringing necessary anyhow. Of course, if a piano has strings which are over 25 years old, the strings have lost their original resiliency and should be replaced in any event. But, considering all the work involved in restringing, it seems foolhardy to use the old and weathered pin block. It is simpler and more logical to make all the components of the tuning and bearing new. But the decision is up to the technician. Some old pianos shape up amazingly well when the tuning pins are simply replaced with pins a size or two larger in stringing.

Remove the tuning pins, either by turning to the left with a small tuning hammer until they come up out of the block, or by using a reverse drill, with tuning pin head attached. The latter is much less laborious, but the speed of the reverse drill is a matter to consider if you are planning to use the old pin block again. High speeds "burn" the hole, which will offer a less satisfactory grip for the new pins.

Removing and cleaning the plate

Check the manner in which the pin block is held to the plate. Remove any holding screws which keep the block in position, usually by going through the plate into the wrest plank. When all securing screws have been removed between plate and block, you are ready to lift the plate.

By using a 1-ton or larger capacity block and tackle or "come along" type of hoist anchored above the piano plate on a beam which will definitely sustain more than 800 pounds, you can lift the plate out of the grand. Rope (not nylon rope, since it stretches considerably) or webbing straps with a 1-ton rating must be secured to the plate in a pattern resembling a Y. This is necessary to smoothly and evenly lift all heavy portions and to keep the plate as level with the piano as possible. Lift and lower a number of times until you are sure there will be no slipping of your webbings, and then raise the 400 to 500 pound plate a few inches above the grand. Roll the grand out from under the plate. Next, lower the plate onto some four-by-four lumber to keep it from touching the floor.

You can refinish the plate by first cleaning the surface with a good cleaner, burnishing with steel wool, and removing all deposits. Then spray the plate with a good quality bronze or gold lacquer. After this has dried, coat with two coats of clear lacquer. If there are black letters or trademarks which you wish to preserve, either coat them first with light oil, or rub them with thinner immediately after the first coat. This removes the first coat from their surfaces. Burnish all the plate-holding bolts with steel wool or a wire wheel, then coat their top surfaces with lacquer. Try to place the bolts in sequence on a board according to the places where they occurred in the piano.

Making repairs and new parts

Remove the pin block, if you wish. If necessary, cut out a new pin block from material sold by suppliers or the manufacturer, exactly duplicating the outline and the routed depressions in the old one. Raise the plate and fit the block temporarily.

Now clean out all accessible portions of the sound board, bridges, and key bed. Repair whatever is necessary on the sound board and the bridges, being guided by previous instructions in this text. Replace any felt which is damaged in the key bed area and, in general, get the case in shape to receive the rebuilding.

Place the pin block in the piano, and refit the plate. There must be no wiggling of the plate under the 20 tons or so of new pressure you are going to apply. Epoxy makes a solid fitting material between plate and new pin block. Some craftsmen prefer to fit the block perfectly to the plate before placing the block in the piano. This is a good idea.

This matter of correctly fitting the pin block to the plate is important, therefore duplicate the old pin block and its setting within the plate contours *exactly*.

Reinstalling the plate

Reversing the procedure used for lifting the plate out of the piano, reinstall the plate, and replace all pin block securing screws, tightening them as far as you can. Replace all units around the plate which hold it to the piano, and tighten solidly all round. Then start at the beginning, and go around once more, taking up any slack which may have occurred after the plate settled.

Some technicians "lower the plate" so as to give more sound board and bridge bearing. I do not think this is a good idea, since the original design of the instrument was right, and if there is sag in the crown of the sound board, lowering the plate will not make the sound board perform as it should; and if the bridges are low, lowering the plate will throw off so many design angles that you may often build in more scale troubles than you can solve. Repair the bridges if they need recapping; recreate the crown of the sound board if it has sagged, and install the plate at the factory-designed position.

Remember your beginning measurements. The plate should now be seated in exactly the same position and to exactly the same measurements against the sides of the case as you originally found it. If there are to be any changes, let them be in the sound board and bridge repairs, and rely on your side measurements against the case (which cannot change).

Drilling tuning pin holes   You can now build a jig for drilling the tuning pin holes. Using a flat, laminated board which will not sag in the middle (a double thickness of pin block material is recommended, or a braced bottom front panel from an old, junked upright), place the board across the grand so that it will be directly behind the grand agraffes and extending from side to side and toward the back of the grand. Use a table model drill press which can be made to run at 600 to 650 revolutions per minute.

The drill press base should be made of wood, and have wedges placed under it in such a way as to assure that the holes you drill in the pin block will be 7° from the vertical, as measured by a straight line extending upward from the top of the agraffes and a straight line measured upward from the tuning pin plate hole. The 7° must be inclined toward the keyboard of the piano. On some pianos the degree of incline may be less or slightly more. But a good rule of thumb is to drill so that the tuning pin cants toward the front edge of the piano by 7°.

Using a pin block bit which corresponds to the size of the pin you intend to install, drill every hole to this precise angle, continuing all the way through the pin block. If you have placed maple bushings in the hollow holes of the plate, drill them as though they were the top surface of the pin block.

If you are not installing a new block, take a .30 caliber rifle brass cleaning brush and run it at this angle down into the holes and back out again. Do not burn the sides of the holes.

Always drill with the same reasonable pressure and speed, in order to get uniform tendings in all holes. Test your results by blocking up under the pin block and driving in one of the pins you intend to use. If it does not give at least 175 pounds of torque without the string attached, use the next size larger pin for these holes.

Once the pin holes are drilled, and you have decided what size pin **Restringing the piano**
you will use for the piano, block up in the area where you intend to start work. Move the jack and plank along as you complete the sections, in order to insure support under the pin plank as you work in a given area. Take the stringing crank, or T lever, and place a tuning pin in its socket. Bring the proper-sized wire for your unison through the agraffe hole corresponding to the position of the string you are about to install, allowing about 2-3/4 in. extra wire beyond the center of the pin block hole. This will give you three turns of wire around the tuning pin when properly installed.

After seating the end of wire in the eye, wrap the wire around the tuning pin. Make three turns around the pin, wedge its bottom in the top of the hole, and drive in with a 2-pound hammer. Take the tuning lever or a small tuning hammer and move the pin rapidly to the left and then to the right a quarter-turn while bearing upwards on the tuning coil lifter. This will establish a neat set of three wires closely spaced and parallel to each other around the pin just below the eye.

Stretch the wire out to the hitch pin (angling it across the proper position on the bridge), around the pin, and back over the bridge up through the next hole in the agraffe and then up to the next tuning pin hole. Allowing the 2-3/4 in. leeway for the coils, cut the wire off, and wrap it around another tuning pin. Wedge the tip of the pin into the hole, and drive it in with the hammer.

Lift your coils; space at the rise between the tuning pin and agraffe, set in proper bearing positions on the bridge, and draw taut. Do not put a heavy stretch on the string at this time. Do not twist the strings while securing them to the pins in the piano. Chalk your hands to avoid early rusting of the strings.

Rosin dusted on the pins before they are placed in the holes will give a better long-term fit, and eliminate jumping and creaking pins.

Continue on in this manner until you have restrung the entire piano. Remember to change wire sizes where applicable, since every six unisons or so the size will probably change. When you come to the single strings which have an ending in their own loops, make the loop as follows: Allow 5 or 6 in. of extra wire for making the loop, and make the loop before putting the string on the tuning pin. Fasten a nail in a vise. The nail should be the same diameter as the hitch pin. Wrap the string smartly around the nail, and then bring the spare end of string over the wire as closely as you can to the nail. Take four turns around the wire with the looped end, wrapping these turns hard against each other. Sometimes a pair of vise-grip pliers assists in keeping a strong pressure pull on the wire. Leave a ''tail'' of wire extending from the last wrap (about 3/4 in. long); then cut off the rest of the wire.

When placing the loop in the piano, make sure that the tail will bear downward against the plate; thus, the tension put on the wire will also increase the tension placed on the wrappings, and help tighten the loop. Proceed from there, up through the agraffes, or under the capo bar and over the bearing bar to the pin, finishing as in other wires. Some technicians use a looping machine, available from supply houses.

Tuning the piano and installing the dampers

Once the piano is restrung, establish a note for middle C somewhat below its standard pitch. Without using the action, pluck each wire as you go up and down from middle C so that you get a steady ascent and descent of approximately one-half step per note. Now take a hard maple hammer shank, or an old drum stick and vigorously rub down all the strings to put some stretch in them and to even them out. ''Chip in'' the scale again. Rub again. Do this four or five times, until little change occurs after the rubbing.

Now resonate middle C at proper pitch and tune the piano without using the action, simply plucking the strings you intend to tune. After this complete tuning, tap the wire at the hitch pins lightly with a screwdriver until seated firmly at the plate. Realign all tuning pin coils. Now insert the string spacer and get all unison wires so that their spacing relative to each other is accurate.

With the completely regulated action installed, tune the piano to A-442. (Not much higher than this, since over-stressing the strings will cause premature failure later. The author does not see much sense in restringing a piano and then tuning the strings beyond their elastic limits). Now space your hammers and unisons so that the hammers strike all three unison strings at the same time. Check to

A gauge for use in setting damper lift flanges in a piano without measuring and with consistent accuracy, made by the author after a model designed by Kenneth Cadell. Note that the outer wooden edge of the gauge is notched. This notch is useful when re-covering keys in keeping the forward edges of the keys the same distance from the fronts of the keys throughout. The gauge is shown in actual use in setting dampers in a grand piano. The tail is set on the key bed and the lip of the gauge is lifting the damper lever to the proper setting. Gauge construction: Maple base about 1 in. high, 3 in. long and 1-1/2 in. wide; countersunk machine screw in the base; 1/8-in. aluminum hard stock with threads cut for machine screw; wing nut to lock adjustment of the aluminum gauge tongue which will rest on the top surfaces of the key tails in a grand.

make sure that all strings are level in each unison. If you find one string higher or lower than the other, you will have to either replace that agraffe or ream out the hole to duplicate the other holes exactly. Where the strings go under the capo bar, further up in the tenor or treble, you may have to smooth out dents which former strings may have made. That is why you have a curved tongued file in your kit.

Remove the action. Take a gauge made out of 3 in. of hard maple about 1 in. high, such as the one illustrated, and set its lip firmly on the tail of the keys when at rest. Since the gauge is 1/8 in. thick at the point where it touches the key tails, placing it in the key bed under the damper flange lifting levers will exactly lift them to the proper point for installing the damper wires.

Install the dampers (exclusive of the bass) with this gauge. Travel the dampers up and down by hand to satisfy yourself that there is proper motion and that they reseat against the unisons. Do not bend the damper wires if at all possible. Using the parallel-jawed lever pliers, align the dampers to the unisons. All damper wires should, of course, be shiny and clean (use steel wool), and the damper hole bushings must be in good condition.

Just in case you find a damper bushing which is unsatisfactory, you can replace it in the the following manner: Tear, don't cut, bushing felt to conform to the pattern used for rebushing flanges. Make it larger, of course, to completely line the hole in the damper wire bushing rail. Place glue on the last portion of the felt, and pull through until there is a small "doughnut" of damper bushing cloth left above the surface. No need to trim too close under the rail, but spread out the "doughnut" to make it appear similar to other bushings in the rail. Let dry. Old bushings which are corroded may be cleaned by careful reaming with an old damper wire or small file type reamer. Do not enlarge the holes.

Now, begin at one or the other end of the bass strings and replace them, allowing three turns on the tuning pins. As you place each bass string on its hitch pin, hold the loop. Then turn the loop one or one and one-half revolutions in the same direction the copper wrap is running on the bass string. Do not overlook this, as it is essential for a resonant bass.

Bring up the bass strings to standard pitch, press down on each one at the center to stretch, then tune to the pitch you have established on the tenor of the piano.

Reinstall the action, again travel the hammers, and watch the lift of the dampers. All should lift the same amount when a key is depressed. Test the sustain pedal, and using the regulation procedures given previously, get the damper action right. Check the sostenuto according to the Baldwin manual.

Tune the piano four more times to A-442.

The piano will need at least three tunings during the first year after it leaves the shop. But if you have done everything necessary to the action, lifted all coils neatly and kept them that way throughout all tunings, spaced the hammers, traveled the dampers and checked all regulation thereafter, this will be a better piano than you may have expected. Even the wire you used is probably of better quality than that originally installed in the piano. Do the work slowly and carefully. Don't attempt shortcuts. You will be able to charge a good price for good work. And you will be proud of your accomplishment.

Replacing dampers

By now you may have a question, "What about the dampers?" Damper replacement is a simple mechanical matter, provided you bear in mind that the factory installation is usually time-consuming since dampers don't just dampen because they are put against the strings. However, if you care to replace the dampers, be guided by the size and shape of those already present, as well as their location and angle.

Do not alter factory settings or bend wires to make your felts work. Instead, fashion the felt dampers so that they work as the original ones did. They are placed in a critical area of the strings for the best possible dampening action. Use the finest damper felt you can buy. The time saved by the use of excellent materials is enormous. Attach the damper felts to the damper heads with aliphatic glue; then you will have some time while the glue is setting to get the dampers working properly and seated in their proper positions on the strings. The author once tried gluing dampers with contact cement. Never again! Use a slow-setting glue.

On rebuilt grands, the new set of dampers makes a pleasing addition to the all-new appearance of the harp and strings. On old uprights, dampers are not so visible, but often must be replaced due to moth damage and other reasons such as hardening of the felt. Sometimes you can rejuvenate old dampers by carefully "skinning" the face layer off them — not with a sharp object, but by fraying the upper edge slightly until you can get a grip on the thin face layer which has hardened against the strings. Peel this off, leaving a new, softer layer to touch the strings.

If this procedure is not adequate, and you replace the dampers on an upright, put glue on the red surface, and position the damper on the unison some little distance above where the wooden damper head rests. Slide the damper down into position, and glue it to the head.

Lesson 13   Developing a successful business

Many tuners forget that no matter how technically proficient a man may be, he will not prosper unless he becomes sales conscious about his business. Obviously, if people don't know you can do the work, they won't be calling on you. Furthermore, if you are not organized efficiently to keep a steady flow of work coming in, you will soon be complaining about slow times.

The following suggestions are based on conversations with successful tuners who are busy most of the time, and often busier than they want to be. What they have learned about business-getting methods should be useful to most of us.

The quickest way to build a list of customers who will be receptive to your reminder that their instruments will again need tuning is to buy their business from a dealer. The word "buy" is used advisedly, since you do not buy, but give a discount to a dealer for the work he turns over to you. Thus, you share with the dealer some of the money you ordinarily charge for your services.

General conditions in the music business world change yearly and often monthly. It is imprudent to establish a flat fee for the store tunings you do for the dealer or to establish a flat rate for the first tuning you do in the customer's home after he buys a piano. Instead, use the discount system, whereby you make a standard charge for all tunings you do, coinciding with the charges made by professionals in the field in your area. Then, you offer a flat discount of 10%, 20%, or

30% to the dealer on the work you do for him. In this way, you are free to move your rates upward or downward, as the case may be, whenever tuning fees change in your general area or nationally. And there is no need to renegotiate fees with the dealer whenever there is a change in the music business.

Of course, you must be fair with the dealer. If he is giving you a good bit of work, and from time to time asks for a favor, such as a tuning on short notice, or Saturday work, it is not unreasonable on his part to expect you to do your best to make him glad that he deals with you. On the other hand, you should get what you are paying for. The dealer should give you first call on all available piano work, without shopping around for a cheaper man who might be in the neighborhood.

One of the saddest things in this business is to hear a dealer say that a certain tuner who is working for him is "spot-tuning" his customers' pianos. That is, the tuner arrives at the customer's home, and proceeds to tell the lady of the house that he is there to make the first free tuning the dealer promised. He proceeds to check the unisons on the piano, touch up the notes which are really noticeable, and then departs, leaving a poorly-serviced piano.

There are 230 to 250 pins in a piano. A tuning consists of the application of the tuning lever on each pin before you are through. Anything else is not worthy of this profession. In addition, the tuner is cheating not only the customer, but the dealer and himself as well. The customer expected to get full tuning and service, for which the dealer is paying. The tuner hopes to add this customer to his list of future clients who need tuning service every six months or yearly. They won't want the tuner back, so everyone loses.

Once you have secured a customer through a dealer by the discount method, it would be wise to treat him and the dealer as though they were important to your future tuning business, which they certainly are.

Keeping records and advertising

Many businessmen use a customer recall system called "The Automatic Secretary." The system consists of a file card box which is divided into the months of the year. After you have tuned a customer's piano, you enter his name, address, all pertinent information about the piano, and the date of the first tuning on a 3-by-5-in. index file card. The card is placed under the month in which you did the tuning. A duplicate card is filed under the month which is six months later than the date of the tuning. Then each month, as you build up your customer file, you remove the cards of the tunings done six months previously and send a reminder notice that it is time to again tune the piano. You follow up the reminder notices with a personal phone call to set the date and time for the tuning.

One of the better ways to make this system work is to mail a standardized reminder notice. These may be printed according to your specifications, or ordered from the Dampp-Chaser Company, whose address appears in supply catalogs. Their reminder card is a fold-over design. It features a reply section on which the client may suggest friends who also may wish to avail themselves of your services.

Yellow-page telephone directory advertising works well in this profession, provided it is neither blatant nor loud, but simply gives your name, address, and phone number, and describes briefly the services you are qualified to do. Of course, it makes good sense to have some blank file cards beside the phone at your business address. Then whoever takes a customer call will be able to write down what you need to know to make this method a permanent part of your tuning business.

The author has found a yearly appointment book to be a necessary part of this system, since it can be near the phone and appointments may be made far in advance. These tuning appointment books are not discarded, but kept permanently to avoid the possibility of overlooking what was done six months or a year previously.

Prospecting new customers

The principal reason why some do not make money at this or any business is that they are not organized to run an efficient prospecting and servicing organization. Prospect names and customers are valuable. This is even more significant when you have paid 20% to 30% of your regular fees to a dealer in order to make initial contacts with customers.

It is difficult to understand why many tuners discard a valuable name and address after doing the first tuning. Each year they must find a new list of customers to sustain their income. Previous and present customers are the best possible source of continued earnings. Thus, one can have a steady flow of tuning appointments month after month. By using the automatic secretary and an appointment book, carrying the original cards with you as you go out to tune, and returning them to the file at the end of the day's work, you develop a system which builds itself up and never loses a customer. Of course, you must do your work well on the piano, too.

As a tuner, you are part of the music field, and it is incumbent upon you to take part in local musical and cultural activities which enhance the public image of the technician and, in general, contribute to a heightened sense of the beauty and value of piano music.

Fortunately, the author has always been interested in music, both as a listener and as a performer. The contacts made at various functions which were attended by cultured people who love music, concerts, opera, and musical clubs, have added materially to his list of clients. They also added to his sense of personal worth and satisfaction. It would be wise to become well known in musical circles in your area. Whenever possible, speak before small music clubs on pianos and their proper service. Always support the musical activities in your church, school, and civic center. Make the acquaintance of teachers and musicians of your area. Your name and face should be familiar to all who are in music in your area.

Do not fear public speaking. If you are interested in your topic, you can speak acceptably, and often well. But never try to pretend to know about things which you have not done or do not understand.

How often should a piano be tuned?

It is generally understood by technicians that the average piano does not stay in perfect tune for longer than 24 hours. The public does not know much about piano tuning. Many manufacturers say that a piano should be tuned about three or four times in its first year. And they suggest two tunings per year thereafter. Of course, fine concert pianos are tuned once or twice before each concert, and thus have scores of tunings per year. A tuner, if he were able to tune his own piano as often as his ears tell him it needs tuning, would do so at least once a month, and maybe once a week.

Music teachers should have their pianos tuned frequently if they are to have the kind of pianos that will train their students' ears to hear sounds in the proper pitch, and pitches within a key in proper relationship to each other. It is true that more pianos go to ruin due to lack of proper service than from any other cause. Neglect ruins a piano. Part of your activities, and your conversations with your tuning customers and dealers should be directed at promoting the idea of proper servicing of pianos if the dealer is to prosper and if the client is to get what he paid for.

Aubrey Willis, who is widely known among piano tuners, once made a tape recording in which he explains "Why Johnny Can't Play." The gist of it is that Johnny listens to TV and hears fine music played by trained musicians on properly tuned pianos. When Johnny's parents purchase the piano, it has an excellent sound. But in the months and years that follow, it is not serviced regularly. So Johnny cannot sound good on it no matter how hard he practices. More and more, his music sounds different from that played on his teacher's piano, and not at all like the music on records and TV.

Johnny thinks he has practiced in vain and is not playing nearly as well as his parents believe he should. His ears are not accustomed to the proper pitches for arpeggios, and when he plays his lesson at his teacher's place, he thinks he is making mistakes when he isn't. He loses interest, and prefers to play baseball or listen to recordings.

The recording goes on to say that if a person who knows something about music and proper pitch should visit Johnny's parents, he might inform them that the piano needs tuning. They would look through the phone book, and then call different tuners, trying to find the cheapest one. If they got him, chances are that the piano would be in worse shape when he was through with it than it was before he began to "gut" it of all musicality. Then, with the action messed up and the sounds which come from the piano resembling nothing musical, Johnny totally gives up.

The piano sits in the living room gathering dust and family pictures. The relatives, who were aware of the piano purchase, and were somewhat envious, now decide that there is no sense in buying a piano because "it is almost impossible to learn to play one." Furthermore, they don't think Johnny's folks were very smart to invest so much money in something which never sounds good. So, the chain of dismay and discontent kills future sales of pianos to Johnny's relatives and future business for competent tuners.

The day will come when better piano manfacturers will warrant their pianos and insist that a portion of the sales price be set aside to service them. When that day comes, your business will depend on your being among the recognized, foremost craftsmen. Until then,

Piano manufacturers and servicing

your business will depend on your selling the idea of piano service by a competent man to all who come in contact with you. Fortunate are you, indeed, if you meet a dealer who sees the picture as it is, and does not consider the tuner as a necessary evil and an expense to minimize as much as possible.

Good piano companies take the trouble to put out service manuals and to maintain a service and technical department. Learn to know these companies and follow their manuals. Keep in close contact with their service departments. This is vital to the future health of your business. These are the companies that will remain viable and in business in the years to come. Dozens of piano manufacturers have gone out of business in recent years. The concerned companies who value piano service and who encourage good technical work and fine tuning will probably be the only ones around in the future.

Tuning pianos in the public schools

There are some men in this business who have built a considerable clientele by bidding on work at public schools. While the author is discouraged by the attitudes of most music department heads and school administrators towards quality piano maintenance, still it is true that there are more pianos in a school than in possibly any other building. If you would like to bid on school business, a letter on your own letterhead asking for the chance to bid on their piano service is usually all that is required. Usually, school system pianos have been sadly neglected, and if worked on at all, have been botched up by a cut-rate mechanic.

If you should contact a school where the pianos have had good service and regular tuning, you know that a good man worked on them. Therefore, there is reason to wonder why the school would want to make a change in their technician unless it was simply a matter of trying to get the lowest-priced man in the area. But do not become the price-cutter. Most intelligent people know that a competent craftsman is worth excellent pay, and if you quote low, they won't have a high opinion of your ability. If you do work cheap, in time you will find that you do it in a cheap way. This will become a fact because you will not be paid enough to warrant spending sufficient time on a project to really do it well.

It is also a fact that many schools never seem to set up a schedule for the tunings except during your busiest season. Furthermore, tuning during school hours is nearly impossible because of the pandemonium. The author has often been just about ready to lower the string to that last whisper beat and caress it into perfect unison when suddenly the gym class roared in, shouting and screaming. A walk outdoors and some moments spent in meditation is possibly the only remedy for the piano tuner in such a case. Even so, your ear is never quite the same for the rest of the day.

Often, you are left standing in a hallway waiting for some event to end or a class to begin. You do not make money standing around in hallways being conspicuous. However, the unusual can happen. It is pleasant to tune a fine grand on the stage of an auditorium or theatre for some special musical program and then be paid promptly instead of waiting 60 to 90 days for your money from a school. Bidding will sometimes get you business; but sometimes you will be giving yourself ''the business'' by bidding.

Since taxes pay for pianos in schools, it is too bad that money is not set aside to cover adequate maintenance of the instruments. Without this care, they become prematurely inoperative.

Tuning pianos
in colleges and churches

The feelings expressed about public school business do not apply to colleges. Some of the most satisfying work in the tuning field is to be found in the music departments of colleges and universities. Some of the finest pianos, as well as some of the most capable administrators and teaching professionals in the world, are found in the universities. Generally these people want fine work and are sufficiently trained to appreciate careful craftsmanship. The music department often employs a full-time staff technician to keep all instruments in excellent repair, and the standards are high.

On occasion, you will be called, not on a bid basis, to tune or repair for junior colleges and other types of institutions. By all means, welcome the chance to work in such surroundings and get to know the professionals who teach there. You will always remember such experiences with pleasant emotions and you will be well paid. As in every case, they deserve your best efforts. The inner satisfaction you will receive will be worth immeasurably more than the fees.

Churches often take a long time to pay you, but this work is comparatively better than public school work. Some of the larger churches have high-quality instruments in their sanctuaries. And, usually, there is a retired klunker or two in the basement or Sunday school rooms. Once you are in a church, if your work is done well and the congregation can appreciate the difference fine tuning makes, the chances are you will have started to build a pretty good future business with other local churches.

Church work is ideal because you do not usually have to bid on the work. Also, church work is satisfying because you are free from noise or interference from other people while you are working, and can fine tune to your heart's content. In addition to this, there is always the joy of preparing an instrument which will be used for worship. Thus, you may bring a new dimension to the hymns and grand old songs of faith which have sustained people down through the ages. The rewards in church work are more than financial.

The importance of working in your own shop

Of course, it makes good sense to always have a piano in your shop which you are rebuilding. Nothing can sustain your morale on those days when tuning work goes badly, or when people fail to be home at the appointed hour. Rebuilding and working on pianos in your own shop enables you to experiment with methods and techniques that you would not have the opportunity to try when out working for the public. In addition, rebuilding pianos enables you to make extra money. This frees you from being dependent solely on tuning for your income. Some tuners, having reached a high degree of technical skill in rebuilding, confine their total efforts to this section of the piano business. They not only rebuild to sell to the public, but renovate dealers' trade-ins, and take care of certain work for other tuners who for one reason or another cannot perform the work they've taken on. Custom work is lucrative.

Professionalism

The proven way to be successful in piano craftsmanship is to perform your work in such a way that it reflects the highest standards of professionalism. Assume that your technique and skill is on a par with that of the better men in your community. Once you have established this attitude, and if your work is commensurate with your standards, you will find that your business will build itself as people begin to realize how good you are at what you do.

Word-of-mouth advertising from satisfied clients is still the most satisfactory way of getting new business. The author knows of one technician who never advertises and yet is busier than he wants to be. This happy state of affairs is due to the fact that the word has gotten around that he is the best man to get for a tuning job in his area. He does not discount to anybody, whether teacher or dealer, and he is not actively looking for business.

Benjamin Franklin once said, "Keep thy shop and thy shop will keep thee." If you bring good work to others, they will bring their tuning jobs to you.

One more word on business-getting methods, and the ways they work for various tuners: It is not possible to run a business which is consistently supplied with customers unless you are organized and ready to move into new circles where you may make contacts with new clients. None of the activities suggested by the author will be useful to you unless you plan your work and then work according to your plan.

Some final tips

One highly-skilled practitioner of this art, who is located in a major city, arranges the next tuning appointment for a particular piano immediately after he finishes a job. He takes out his book and makes the next appointment on the spot, telling the client he will send a reminder notice a week before he shows up to tune the piano. This tuner is always busy. He follows through on his plan, sends the reminder, or calls on the phone, and locks up his business so that he has it all scheduled a year or so in advance. Of course, he does fine work for every client. And he does fine work in his own interests as well, by being well organized.

I know of a tuner who used the card file system but kept it with him on calls. One day it was stolen from the seat of his car while he was inside a home tuning a piano. There was a flaw in his organization: He should have carried cards of only those tuning jobs he was to do on a particular day.

Don't rely on your memory. Have your information in writing. It is practical to buy a cassette tape recorder and carry it with you on jobs. This provides a handy way of "making notes," eliminates the dangerous practice of trying to write while driving, and gives more detail when replayed than any hastily made note would give.

Estimates on rebuilding jobs recorded on tape are more detailed and easier to refer to later. Another advantage of the tape recorder is that the good ideas which occur to every person at one time or another can be preserved to guide your future planning and thinking.

While your thoughts may not be immortal, they might be worth saving for a week or so at least! Here is an electronic secretary whose memory never fails.

Business cards may be purchased from supply houses. A business card also serves as a reminder when you leave one in the music bench of the piano. Some place the card inside the piano, but it is doubtful anyone except another tuner would find it there. Put your card in the bench, and then tell the client where you put it. Things stay in piano benches a long time. Dignity should be the watchword when choosing words to print on your cards. Let your business card present the proper image.

Leave some printed information on piano care on the music desk of the piano when you are done with a job, or present it to the client. You can write it yourself. Even a mimeographed sheet will do. Have your imprint on the brochure.

Maintain your image

More business will result from the appearance you present before the public and your clients than from any other source. A man in this profession should visualize the kind of attire he would like to see on a first-class piano tuner. That is, he should have a suitable wardrobe. He should dress up to the image of professionalism, not down from it. Professional technicians should dress like professionals. Uniforms, while often neat, do not present the image of a man who is viewing his work as an art. They suggest the wearer is a man who is just doing a job.

Some highly skilled trades do require uniforms which, when soiled, can be readily washed. Ours is not one of these trades. We can dress well and we should. And remember the details: Keep your shoes shined. Many housewives judge a man by the shine of his shoes. There's nothing wrong with wearing a tie, either.

Among piano craftsmen are M.D.'s, Ph.D.'s, and artists of the concert stage. Ours can be a high and noble profession. But we will have to believe it if we want others to believe it.

Lesson 14 Tuning electronic organs and pianos

As a tuner, you may be asked to tune a piano to a Hammond organ. Churches, schools, and even private homes often have both instruments. To clarify the method of tuning required, it helps to know a few things about the Hammond organ.

Hammond organs have a synchronous motor which spins a series of tone wheels in a magnetic field, and the individual tones thus created are then amplified. A Hammond does not need tuning. Sometimes service is needed for the sound volume pedal, which is a set of metallic capacitor blades moving inside another set of base blades and thus varying the capacity. Cleaning this unit (and making sure that there are no foreign particles in it) usually clears up a scratchy sound. The amplifiers, too, can go out of order, and require new tubes, capacitors, and resistors. In addition, the pickup circuits sometimes are damaged.

The Hammond offers one frequency which is exactly on pitch with tuning concert A. A-440 is generated by the A-440 key. All the other Hammond frequencies differ slightly from a standard tempered octave. When the vibrato is turned on, or a Leslie speaker is hooked up to the Hammond, the tones rise and fall a few cycles on either side of concert pitch. For this reason, do not attempt to tune to a Hammond unless all vibrato and Leslie controls are turned off.

Turn on the Hammond, and turn off all voicing tablets except the one which gives the clearest flute tone. Using a rubber wedge mute,

189

depress and keep down the key corresponding to A-440. Then, using that tone as your base reference, tune the piano A to it. Complete a standard temperament on the piano and proceed to tune it completely. The piano will sound as it should when played alone. Also, the Hammond will still sound as it should. And the two instruments, when played together, will be compatible. This is all you can do when asked to tune a Hammond and a piano so that they can be played together.

Obviously the vibrato on the organ will cover up the slight discrepancies which may exist between the temperaments of the two instruments.

Do not calibrate the whole octave on a Strobotuner and then proceed to tune the piano to this standard. The piano will sound horrible when played alone. And the two instruments will not sound any better when played together.

Tuning other organs   Most other organs can be divided into individual oscillator models and Formant organs. The individual oscillator organ is precisely what the name implies. Each tone on the organ is produced by an independent oscillator. Gulbransen and other well-made organs use this system. In these organs, you are confronted with a bank of oscillators which must be tuned individually to each key. Fortunately, the tuning slugs, which move an iron core up and down within the core of the oscillator coil, are plainly marked as to the key they respond to.

To tune these organs, it is practically a necessity to use a Strobotuner for calibration or a Peterson chromatic tuner so as to have a fixed standard to beat the output of the oscillator against. It is next to impossible to tune an even temperament as you do in a piano, since the harmonic content of organ tones is not the same as those encountered in piano tuning. When you find such an organ, and if it is necessary to play it with a piano, tune the piano correctly, and then tune the organ to it. Do not tune the piano to the organ; if you do, you will not have an equal temperament on either instrument.

With calmness and care, it is possible to tune these organs and do a good job. The pedal generators are not tied in exactly to the tone of the first pedals proceeding upward from low C to G. Instead, the fractions of the C tone generated by the lowest C oscillator on the organ, and the fractions of the G tone, are beat together to produce a

left:

A view of the back of an independent tone generator organ shows the 84 tone oscillators and their tuning slug ends. All notes are clearly marked on the face of the oscillator boards. They are staggered, as you may note, from one board to the next. A Leslie tremolo unit is seen at the lower left.

right:

A Formant-type organ uses master oscillators for top tone in each series (C1, C2, C3, C4, C5, etc.). Tuning cans are for the purpose of tuning the top note in each series, after which the electronic divider circuits complete the tuning of all Cs in the organ, and so on. Notice that this is a tube-type organ, but transistor types using this same circuit design are tuned in the same way. The basic master oscillator concept is used, and when tuning, it matters little whether you are tuning a tube-type organ or a transistorized one; the tuning works out the same.

tone somewhat removed from either, and give the aural impression of a low C being played on the organ.

If the lowest C is properly tuned according to the strobe, and the lowest G is thus tuned, you can alter any objectionable beats between the two when the pedal is depressed by removing half the interference in each tuning slug. This is true for all the lower foot pedal notes up to G, and their respective component oscillators.

These organs do go out of tune because of changes which take place in their electronic components when used over the years. You may be asked to tune them. In setting up the organ for tuning, turn off all tremolo or vibrato. Turn off all stops except the highest flute stops and begin from there. When the sounds become confusing to your ear in the lower part of the flute section, shut off the first tab you used, and turn on the next lower flute section. These steps are not nearly as confusing as they seem.

Formant organs

Formant organs operate on a slightly different principle than the ones just discussed. These organs are so designed that the highest tone of any note is the fundamental oscillation. This means that, for example, the tuning coil with its movable slug, or a transformer with its variable air gap, directly controls the top C. The next C down is automatically tuned when the top C is tuned. Thus, all notes which are C are tuned at the same time. The reason for this is that the Formant organ uses divider circuits to divide the top oscillator tone, and has a series of divider circuits in each bank of oscillator units which cuts the error in half all the way down through the organ. Thus, there are only 12 main oscillators to tune. All other tones are obtained by division from these can-type tuning units. A long, hexagonal tuning wand, such as the type used to adjust trimmers in radios, is employed in most of such units to move the oscillator slugs.

Again, it is very difficult to set a temperament on Formant organs. The best method is to use a strobe or chromatic tuner, and then count on the organ itself to tune the rest of the octaves after you have tuned the top notes. Volume controls on these organs give trouble, and are usually simple variable resistors such as you find on radios. They are turned by means of the foot pedal (volume control) linkage.

Older Thomas organs employ a combination system, wherein each transformer with its variable air gap influences three notes. In addition, there are individual trimmers adjacent to the transformers (and readily identified) for each of the three other notes. The pedal system must be tuned as well. Complete instructions for its tuning are found prominently displayed on top of the pedal rack, and if followed, present no difficulty.

In some of the more recent stereo-type organs, both controlled oscillators, which control the tones submitted to the lower dividers, and independent tone generator systems are used. The tibia organ is an independent type, and the accompanying main organ is of the Formant divider type. You have, in effect, two organs to tune.

When you tune an organ, do not make the mistake of quoting a price less than your regular piano tuning fee. The organ may have as many as 84 separate oscillators for you to tune. If it is a Formant organ, of course, you will have fewer oscillators to tune but you may find that the customer expects you also to look into the trouble he may have been having with the volume pedal, and that scratchy noise he hears when he flips on a certain stop tablet. So, charge as you would for piano work, or more. Then, if you must, proceed slowly because some organs have ingenious means of securing the back, involving interlock cords, etc., and various moving parts, such as built-in Leslie tremolo systems.

By all means, contact the local dealer and avail yourself of a service manual on the various makes of organs before you get too deeply involved with them. The manuals are usually dependable and often offer better ways of doing things than your mind might devise. Have no qualms about possible troubles in tuning organs. They are all tuned in one of the three ways described in this lesson.

Pipe organs have individual pipes which are keyed either mechanically or electrically to operate from ranks or wind chests which supply the pipes with power. Basically, the big blower furnishes wind power to the bellows. Various take-off pipes deliver portions of the bellows power to the individual chests. It is not a good idea to get into this work until you have studied pipe organs in some of the many books available on the subject. First of all, organ maintenance for these large units requires considerable agility. In addition, you must be willing to accept ear-splitting sounds while you are working in the main chest room tuning the pipes.

Pipe organs

Some of my friends are pipe organ specialists or were until their hearing left them. The author has tuned these monsters, and found there is nothing to it, since you are only matching the pipes against a fixed standard tone, and then octaving out through the rank of pipes. However, when you are called to match the pipe organ and piano, make sure that some qualified man has come, or will soon come, to tune the pipe organ. Then, you go in and tune the piano to the A-440 or A-435, which is the standard pitch he will use on the organ. Tune the piano as a piano, and don't attempt to make it match the organ in intervals. Pianos are different from organs.

It takes two people to tune a pipe organ. Once the key is depressed, the tuner must climb around in the chest room while shouting instructions to the helper at the console. The sustained tones cannot be softened in the chest room, since volume control is a matter of opening and closing shutters from the chest room to the main auditorium. Stay out of those rooms if you would like to continue hearing fine beats in pianos.

At this point, a true story may illustrate why it is better to tune an organ to a well-tuned piano than to tune a piano to an organ. A close friend of the author's, and a man who is also one of the finest concert tuners in America, was called to tune a new piano for a public presentation concert by a well-known television personality. This performer was to demonstrate a certain company's products, including their pianos and organs.

The tuner tuned the piano to concert pitch, using the time-tested aural method. The artist appeared for rehearsal and complained that the piano was not right, since he was to play it with the organ. The tuner said little, but returned at the dealer's request and again carefully tuned the piano. After all, this tuner knew, as all tuners should know, that a piano could possibly change its tune due to atmospheric conditions which might have been different in the auditorium from what they had been in the dealer's showroom. Again he was informed that the artist did not like the way the piano sounded with the organ.

The tuner suggested that the head of the organ service at the dealership tune the organ to match the piano. Unfortunately, due to the tuner's refusal to tune the piano again, the organ man had to tune the organ at three in the morning. But tune it to the piano he did! The concert was performed the next day. Beautifully.

The author's family purchased an album from the artist's representative at the concert hall. This album included all the demonstration pieces for organ and piano which were included in the public performance. When we listened to the album at home, we discovered that much of what we heard in tone during the concert was missing from the album. We checked with other people who had attended the concert and who had bought the album. We found that they, too, were missing something that they heard at the concert. Then we listened to the artist's weekly show on TV. Again, we found the concert had something more thrilling in sound than the playing of piano and organ did on TV. It seems that the ear of the fine concert tuner was able to set a more musically satisfying temperament and carry it out throughout the piano than electronic organ temperament could do. Once the organ was tuned to a finely tuned piano, both instruments had a thrilling sound, whether played alone or together.

Perhaps some of the delicate nuances which the audience enjoyed at the live performance were lost on records and television. Or perhaps the fact that the organ was originally tuned by electronic standards made it impossible to match an aural temperament to it. Certainly, it was necessary that both instruments be tuned to one standard to get the best tonal results.

Tune the piano. Then, if necessary, tune the organ to it. If this is impossible, as on a Hammond or pipe organ, tune the A to the organ, and then tune the piano precisely as always. You will be glad you did. So will the listeners. The human ear is a wonderful "tool."

Tuning electronic pianos

Electric pianos are commonly used today for group teaching purposes. Determining the method to follow for tuning is rather simple. Some electric pianos have an action much like that of a regular piano. Most electric pianos produce their tone by having the hammer strike some object, such as a tuned reed, taut string, or metal plate. The sound which is produced by this action is then picked up by a transducer (similar to capacitor microphone) and carried through the input lead to the amplifier (which is a standard audio amplifier). A volume control is connected in series with the input lead, or on the grid circuit of one of the tubes, or in the transistor keying circuit of the transistor amplifier, depending on whether the piano uses tube circuits or transistors.

If the piano tone is produced by metallic reeds moving in a small resonant space, adding weight to the reeds decreases their frequency of pitch, and lightening the tips increases their pitch. When it is necessary to replace a reed, order it from the manufacturer by its number. If the replacement (and they do break) requires extra weight, liquid solder or the application of hot solder with a small soldering iron will over-weight the reed. You then trim off the excess with a fine file until you have the pitch you desire. Obviously, the reverse process is used if you want a higher tone than the reed is producing.

Recently, Baldwin began to manufacture an electronic piano which uses a piano action (especially designed for this unit), and a cast iron harp, with pin block, tuning pins, strings, and dampers. This piano is an interesting unit in that the tension on the strings is not as great as is required in a regular piano. This, of course, is because no sound board is used, and the tone is picked up from the strings by an electronic microphone (transducer), which runs the entire bottom length of the harp. Special instructions for regulating exist for this piano, and can be acquired from the Baldwin Company. In effect, it has an underhammer action with standard keys and rails. Many modern plastic components have made some parts of the action somewhat different from what the technician is used to, and therefore securing a service manual is a good idea. Tuning is accomplished in much the same manner as tuning a standard piano. However, the author feels that a Strobotuner is definitely an aid in tuning this instrument since the strip muting possibilities are not as feasible as in a regular piano. The piano is tuned from the back.

Measurements used in tuning the electric piano

As far as the tuner is concerned, this piano is easier to tune than a regular piano. The tone is remarkably true to piano tone. Many colleges use these instruments in teaching large groups. No doubt, homes and entertainment places will find this an easy piano to buy and to move around readily. For that reason, it would be a good idea to learn as much as you can about it. Temperament can be set on this piano, and aural tuning is definitely possible.

The tops of the natural keys should be about 2-9/32 in. above the top of the key bed on this piano. The sharps should be 15/32 in. above the white keys. Standard key travel is 13/32 in. Use punchings, just as in all pianos, to set this depth. The hammer stroke should be 15/16 in. to 1 in. maximum from rest position to contact with the strings. Adjust the stroke with a screw in the hammer butt. Jacks should follow the hammer butt when it is moved away by about 3/32 in. If there is too much or not enough movement of the jack, the wippen arm supporting the jack spring should be bent slightly. There is a special tool available for this purpose. *Don't bend any springs.* Lifting all the hammer butts will allow the jacks to move slightly, but if the jack moves too far, the butts will not drop freely.

Let-off can be checked as follows: Depress the key slowly until the spoon trips the lower arm of the jack, allowing the jack to move from

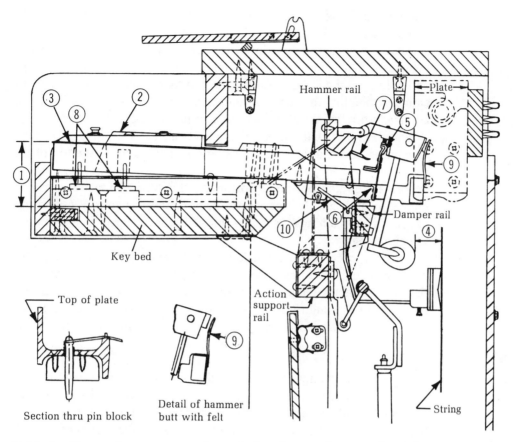

Key bed

Hammer rail

Plate

Damper rail

String

Action support rail

Top of plate

Section thru pin block

Detail of hammer butt with felt

Baldwin Electropiano parts and regulation instructions. Follow the sequence as listed when attempting regulation. Note that the tuning pin eyes which hold the coil are on the opposite end of the tuning pin from the point where the technician places his tuning lever. However, tension on these pianos ranges from 55 to 75 pounds, so tuning is relatively easy.

Regulation and adjustment: Top of natural key 2-9/32 in. above 1-in. key bed (1); set sharps 15/32 in. above natural key (2); lay touch 13/32 in. — measure 1/4 in. back from front of key (3); set blow 15/16 in. to 1 in. (4); adjust jack spring preload 3/32 in. approximately (5); bend wippen at (6) to set jack to center line of butt screw with hammer 1/16 in. from string — do not bend spring; set let-off 1/16 in. to 3/32 in. by bending spoon (7); set key travel after let-off to .040 in. (after-touch) (8); set back check 5/16 in. (9); dampers start to lift with hammer at 1/2 in. from string (bend wire) (10).

underneath the screw in the hammer butt. The distance between the hammer tip and the strings at let-off should be 1/16 in. to 3/32 in. A suitable gauge is the pickup finger from a Howard piano, which measures .096 in. in diameter. Make a right-angle bend on the end and hold it on the strings. Adjust the hammer to let-off as it meets the gauge by bending the spoon slightly. Now the entire hammer action is adjusted with the possible exception of the back check.

It is desirable that the after-touch on all keys be alike. To spot-check this, insert a .040-in. punching under the key on the top of the front felt washer; push the key down, and observe where the let-off occurs as the key bottoms. Bottoming should occur just as the butt begins to drop and just as let-off occurs. If the hammer butt drops too far, add punchings under the felt. If it doesn't drop at all, remove the punchings.

The back check is an extension of the wippen, and can be adjusted by slight bending. Adjust it to stop the checked hammer 5/16 in. from the strings. If bent back too much, the hammer will not stop, but drop through; repetition will also be faulty. When the hammers are checked at 5/16 in. from the string, the hammer action is in regulation.

The damper action is very simple. When the sustain pedal is depressed, the damper rod moves the dampers back away from the strings as in conventional pianos. To make all of the dampers start together, adjust the position of each damper head on the damper wire by loosening the damper head screw, sliding the damper head back or forth, and retightening the screw.

To regulate the damper to the key, note first that the wippen has a sleeved peg that lifts the damper wire when a key is played. This end of the damper wire corresponds to the spoon on a conventional piano. It can be bent to adjust the damper lift on each individual note. There are various tools available for this adjustment and choice depends upon your preference. Either regular Baldwin bending pliers or back-check bending pliers can be used. The damper wires are readily accessible from below the key bed with the lower frame removed. The damper motion should be 3/16 in. to 1/4 in. in the bass range to make sure the V of the damper clears the string entirely. In the treble range, 3/16-in. motion is quite enough. When the hammer is approximately halfway (1/2 in.)to the string, the damper should start into motion.

Should damper disassembly be required for any reason, snap the damper wire out of the damper flange. When replacing it, snap the damper pivot wires into the flange and swing the damper spring back into place over the damper wire.

Single keys can be removed from this action. Use care to avoid bending the jack spring or enlarging the balance pin hole. To remove a single key, first remove the hammer butt assembly by removing the flange screw, raising the butt, turning it sideways, and passing it through the wippen. This frees the key for removal as follows: Work the jack spring between the spoons, under the hammer rail, and then lift the key up and out. In the reverse process, flex the jack spring down beneath the hammer rail when replacing the key.

When you need to remove many keys, it is simpler to remove the entire hammer rail. This is not difficult. Remove the piano back. Disconnect the input plugs. Remove the bottom plate screw. Tilt the bottom of the plate outward, moving the strings away from the dampers, and lift the plate out of the mounting brackets. Rotate the hammers upward between the wippens until they rest upon the back checks. Remove the hammer rail bracket screws and lift the rail. (A rod under the hammer shanks will facilitate removal.) To replace the hammer rail, reverse the above steps.

The above instruction on the Baldwin Electropiano is important to you as a technician, since this instrument differs from all other pianos in some ways but is close enough to standard piano design that you will be glad to work on it. No doubt you will be working on many of these pianos as the years roll by.

The day of electronic pianos is here and the possible market staggers the imagination. If manufacturers make a piano that continues to sound like a piano, weighs less, does not have the tension difficulties that most small pianos have, and can be listened to with earphones, the sale of these units to homes should be great. All that remains is for the technician to get to know these units and learn to bring out the best sound he can from them.

Lesson 15 Basic troubleshooting and repair of organs

As outlined before, electronic organs may be of several types: a basically independent tone generating system with the basic tones amplified; Formant designed circuits, with divider networks producing harmonics of the fundamental oscillator frequency; or a tone wheel system, such as the Hammond. In some older units, the tone was also generated by a wind chest, with various vibrating reeds, in which vibrations were picked up by a transducer microphone system. While these units went out of production some years ago, you still will find many of them in older churches. Furthermore, recent improvements in plastic reed design have made it possible for similar tone systems to be incorporated in some of the newer electronic organs. Thus, we find the oldest style of organ again coming to the front as the latest model.

If you are to go into organ servicing in a serious way, it is advisable to take a course in basic electronics, or to at least get a copy of the *Radio Amateur's Handbook*, which is offered under the auspices of the American Radio Relay League. It details circuitry in a very basic way. It is difficult to repair electric organs without a good working knowledge of radio and electronic theory. Many of the recent organs have extremely sophisticated circuitry, incorporating computer logic circuits, transistorized gate systems, and feed-back circuits. A sound background in electronics is essential to do a first class job on them.

However, basic troubleshooting and repairs can be done while you are gaining additional theoretical knowledge. To begin, you will need all the pliers and screwdrivers used in piano work, and in addition, a good 40-watt soldering iron, a 150-watt soldering iron, a mutual conductance tube tester, a vacuum tube voltmeter, and if you are to make satisfactory progress, a portable oscilloscope. Buy quality equipment. Always read the manuals that accompany test equipment. Many fine techniques of servicing electronic instruments are outlined in these manuals and they will make electronic work easier.

The usual electronic organ is basically designed so that the amplifier is "on" when the organ is turned on. In the independent generator organ, the voltages from the basic power supply, which is an integral part of the amplifier, are made available to the keying circuits. Once a key is depressed, a circuit is established between the oscillator and the supply voltage fed to it by the amplifier. The oscillator instantly generates its proper signal. The signal coming from the oscillator is then fed into a voicing or straf circuit, which colors the tone produced by the basic oscillator.

The coloring desired is selected by the use of stop tablets which may be above or surrounding the keyboard. Once the stop has been depressed, the tone generated by the oscillator passes through the coloring circuits of the straf unit, and from there to the amplifier (going into the amplifier at the input terminal or connection). Inside the amplifier, the signal is amplified to a level which will move the speaker or speakers. The tone passes through the output circuits of the amplifier, and is carried to the speakers. It causes the speaker cones to move backward and forward at the frequency of the tone applied.

The speaker cone, in its movement, excites the air in the area in front of the speaker. This movement of air impinges upon the human ear, causing us to hear the sound produced by the organ. In some cases, the movement of "speaker air" is interfered with by a rotating drum, with specially designed apertures, which causes the air to be impacted and expanded with the rotation of the interfering drum. In effect, this is the basic principle of the "Leslie tone" system. The sound reaching the human ear is thus changed and arrives in discernible pulses.

The volume of sound is controlled by a foot lever which either moves a small lamp closer to a light-sensitive conductor, or by a rheostat which corresponds closely to the volume control on a radio or TV set. The circuits for this expression of volume control are connected directly to one preamplifying stage of the master amplifier, thus controlling the complete volume of the stage of amplification, or are connected to the input circuit of the amplifier, bringing the output of the oscillators through the volume control before the oscillations arrive at the amplifier.

In the Formant organ, the amplifier and the master power supply in the amplifier function in much the same way. However, in the Formant organ, the oscillators are continuously keyed by voltage from the amplifier, and in effect, are playing all the time. The necessity for this is clear, when we remember that the fundamental oscillator must function before the divider networks can produce the harmonics. The stop tablet works in precisely the same manner as in the independent organ, but the output of the oscillators is connected to the keying circuits. Thus, the output of continuously playing oscillator circuits is channeled through the key or depressed keys into the volume control, and into the input circuit of the amplifier.

In the case of the vibrating reed organ, the wind chest operates and the reeds vibrate at all times when the organ is turned on. The individual transducer mikes are connected to the keying circuits, and depressing the key simply connects the output of the reed mike to the amplifier, after passing the tone through the stop or straf tablet circuits. This is true of the tone wheel organ as well.

By far the largest percentage of trouble in electronic organs can be diagnosed if you get the working concept of the organ firmly fixed in your mind. Study the block diagrams of the basic organ set-ups; it will become obvious where the more frequent difficulties occur.

Recently, organs which incorporate both systems of tone production have come on the market. They provide both a tibia organ and a main organ which can be played separately or together in the one instrument. This does not confuse the technician who simplifies the system into block diagrams, since he can then determine which organ (for there are essentially two organs in one cabinet in this case) is defective. He may then proceed to fix the organ, being guided by circuit characteristics of the particular type he is working on.

Since the fuse is the weakest part of an electrical circuit, common sense suggests that blown fuses will be the most common source of malfunction. It works out that way. Fuses are located in accessible places in organs, plainly marked, and their ratings noted. Do not replace with a fuse rated higher than the one installed by the

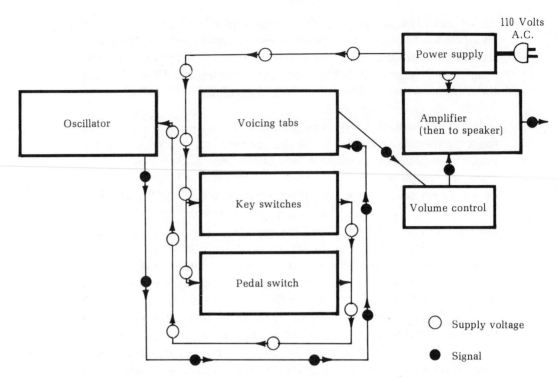

Block diagram of the basic circuits in the independent tone gener-ating organ, with associated controls.

manufacturer. If the replacement fuse blows at once, then you must assume that there is a breakdown in the circuit or circuits which that fuse protects. From this point on, it is a matter of finding out what is causing too much voltage to be applied or too much current to be consumed in a particular circuit.

The test unit to be used here is the vacuum tube voltmeter. Often there is a short between one component and another, or in a plastic circuit board. By carefully disconnecting each section, and beginning at the section closest to the fuse, you can usually isolate the section which is causing the difficulty. Then it is a matter of finding the component in the section which is faulty.

Most units of organs can be disconnected from the main power supply by unplugging them. To continue this illustration, if all units are disconnected from the main amplifier and power supply, and the fuse still blows, then the defect is in the main amplifier and power supply. Avail yourself of a schematic of the amplifier and power supply, and using your test meter, read the voltages at the various points indicated by the manufacturer. By making careful voltage readings, all conditions of the circuits can be determined. Don't jab screwdrivers and metallic objects into electrical circuits. You will destroy components and cause shorts which will be harder to fix than the orginal problem you encountered.

Second in weakness to the fuses in an organ are the tubes which function in the various circuits. In tube organs, therefore, it is advisable to be guided by the manufacturer's service manual when checking and substituting the various tubes in the organ. Of course, the use of the tube tester is clearly indicated when all seems normal, but one circuit in a tube organ is not functioning perfectly or at all. Do not rush to plug in a tube that "looks just like the one you removed." Unless the old tube is replaced by a tube having exactly the same number, you will be in big trouble. For example, in some older organs, a series of 6x8 tubes is used for some oscillator circuits. Many tubes look just like a 6x8, but nothing else will work in that circuit.

Block diagram of the basic circuits of the Formant organ, with associated controls. Note that the keying circuits perform different functions in this organ from those in the independent tone generating organ.

This holds true for all critical oscillator circuits. Suppose a tube gets red hot, and you replace it with a new one like the others surrounding it. If the new tube also gets red hot, there is something wrong in the circuitry encompassing it. Just because a tube does not glow at all does not necessarily mean that it is bad. And just because a tube lights up does not mean that it is good.

It is possible that the technician, in thinking about transistors, will assume that they take the place of tubes in newer circuits. This is true, so far as it goes. But it does not go far! Tubes are the second weakest point in electronic organs. But transistors are usually more dependable than all the rest of the circuitry. The life expectancy of some transistors under normal conditions of use can range in the neighborhood of 93 years. Suspect the transistor last!

Volume control

After fuses and tubes, consider the volume control. Used more than any other single part of the organ, the volume control is not usually made to stand up to constant use. Scratchy noises, cracks and pops, distortion, and a multitude of other defects which seem to come from the organ in most cases can be isolated in a faulty volume control. Proper repair is not to clean the rheostat, but to replace it with a factory duplicate. Also, the wiring which leads to and from the volume control is often installed in such a way as to be under conditions of almost constant flexing. Finally it shorts out to some other wire or to its own surrounding shield, or it breaks inside the insulation although it doesn't appear broken. Again, the voltmeter, when set so as to measure resistance, will check out wires for you, and tell you if there is continuity within them.

Stop tablets and switches

The next most usual source of malfunction is the stop tablets and their associated switches. From rough or constant use, these will become sloppy, corroded, or damaged in their action. It is unnecessary to dash wildly all over the organ to find the trouble. Sit at the console or keyboard and try the keys, beginning at the lowest one on any manual, with one stop tablet turned on. Go all the way up the keyboard with this one stop on. Then turn it off and turn on the next stop tablet, and repeat the process all the way up the keyboard. This is the way to check stop tablets. It is also the best possible way to check out most systems in the organ.

You can picture in your mind just what is happening as you connect the oscillator to one stop and the next. Then, if the oscillator comes through on some stops and not on others, you won't be tempted to tear into the oscillator circuits, since the oscillator is not at fault. Further, more problems are solved by first spending 10 minutes at the keyboard than by doing your analysis from inside the guts of the organ. Use your brains before you use your tools.

Diodes

In modern transistorized organs, the components which most often cause trouble are the diodes. This is true because transistor circuitry depends to a great extent on the multitudinous use of diodes to control keyed voltages supplied to the circuits. Voltages in transistor circuitry are much lower than the voltages required in tube circuitry. While this eliminates heat problems which cause components to deteriorate in tube circuitry, it also creates a situation whereby a slight change in a component which might not interfere with its function in a tube circuit will cause malfunction in a transistor circuit. The tolerances are far more critical in these circuits. "Close to" values just won't do. Each component replaced must be replaced with one of exactly equal value if all is to function as designed.

Diodes basically are small electrical units which pass current in one direction only. Some of them look like small, swollen wires; others are round pieces of glass enclosing silicon. Still others are button-shaped. Circuit pictorial diagrams and schematics are available from the manufacturer and must be used if you are to do any kind of service work on transistor organs. There is no short cut in transistor circuitry knowledge. The only way to do repairs well on transistor units is to get a good background in electronics and in reading schematics. Then, attend the field seminars offered by manufacturers, where the best men in their field explain the peculiar circuitry of their organs. Wurlitzer offers some of these seminars for both piano and organ technicians two or three times a year. A Wurlitzer dealer can arrange your attendance.

Circuits

Do not use a cheap meter on transistor circuits. First of all, the values of some components run so high that only a good vacuum tube voltmeter will have resistance ranges high enough to measure them accurately. Second, unless you use a good VTVM, you will load the circuits while testing and thus extend errors from your probe into your diagnosis.

The basic difficulties with pedal circuits usually result from broken or damaged switches in the pedal circuits. Look for these first. In transistorized organs, the "gate circuits" take the place of switches, and the diodes in these circuits are the next most frequent source of malfunction. Diodes break easily, and heavy vibrations can cause damage. If you drop one, you can destroy it internally. Heat is sure death to transistors and diodes. Always use a small soldering iron in transistor circuitry repair, and clamp the wire with your surgeon's locking pliers halfway between the place where solder will be applied and the main body of the transistor or diode. This makes a heat dam and protects the part from damage while you are soldering it in place.

In every case, have faith in the circuits as designed by the manufacturer. After all, thousands of dollars are spent in design circuitry, and most organs will work as they should if you believe the manufacturer knew what he was doing. Loose wires, or poorly soldered ones, resulting from slipshod work at the factory and from poor quality control inspection, constitute the reasons for 40% of your repair work as an organ repairman. Parts which have literally "worn out" from heavy use or inconsiderate pounding by a child will be the reason for another 30% of the repairs you will be asked to make. Switches, as part of the voicing tablet controls, and as part of the keying system, will cause another 15%.

Some final tips   Once in a while you will come across an organ which has been tampered with by someone who had a little radio instruction in the army. In this organ, some tubes will be plugged into the wrong places, some diodes may be ruined by hot soldering, or some wires will be connected wrong. But the circuit will work when you restore it to the manufacturer's design, and replace the ruined parts. These defects, along with loose speaker mountings, worn out Leslie belts, and rugs which press up against the pedals and won't let them go down, will make up the reasons for the last 15% of repairs.

Much of what makes an organ work is so tied up with simple mechanical switches, volume controls (mechanical-electric), keying switches, and moving pedals, that a good sense of how things function mechanically will be extremely helpful in repairing. Mechanical devices in organs tend to break more frequently than electrical ones do, because they receive much of the power from the player's hands and feet. The electrical parts have to contend only with their proper voltages and currents unless something mechanical influences them and their surroundings.

Electricity is invisible to the naked eye, unless generated in such quantities that it jumps across an air gap. Therefore, even with considerable theoretical knowledge and familiarity with circuitry, it may be supposed that much agonized thinking about what is happening in a circuit could be eliminated if a man could see what happens. For this and other reasons, a visible means of tracing circuits is the most efficient means of troubleshooting electrical equipment. While the oscilloscope will not take the place of *understanding* what is happening in a circuit, it will certainly make it possible for a technician who is hunting for a malfunction in a circuit to find it quickly.

Using the oscilloscope in organ troubleshooting

The manual which comes with a scope makes it possible for you to calibrate the instrument to accurately measure voltages from their source all the way through a circuit to each component they supply, and through those components to check on the other side of a diode, resistor, condenser, etc., to determine if the circuit component has performed as it should. Miniscule voltages, such as those differences found in transistor circuits under operation and at rest, can be read easily. In addition, the voltages can be measured by an oscilloscope without much possibility of your probe adding voltages to a circuit which could damage the tiny components found there.

Another advantage in using a scope is that you can determine the exact waveform which is being revealed by an oscillator, compare it with the waveform of properly functioning oscillators in the organ, and localize troubles by determining at which point the waveform is altered improperly by some component. With the scope, you start at the oscillator in a Formant organ, trace the pattern into and through the output of each divider section, and compare with the adjacent system for accuracy. If a divider has gone bad, you won't have to wonder which one it is. You'll know at a glance.

From the divider, you trace the signal to the straf or stop tablet units, into and through the applicable switch, all the while seeing the waveform as it is colored and also touching the coloring unit circuit to determine if a stop is offering any output or modifying channel to

A portable oscilloscope may be used for electronic organ trouble-shooting and repairs. The two-position probe which can be used with this instrument prevents loading of circuits and is adequate for all measurements required in organ repair. The scope manual offers extensive operating and calibrating instructions for every kind of audio measurement and diagnosis.

the basic oscillation fed into it. From the straf unit, the tone can be seen proceeding into the volume control, or into the amplifier, after passing through the key switch. At each stage of amplification within the amplifier, you can watch the gain in signal strength, or any distortion introduced by that particular stage, right on out to the output section, and through that into the terminals of the speaker.

For the independent generator organ, the same process is usable, but altered so as to reveal the signal path in accordance to the slightly different course it pursues.

Gate circuits, straf units, even rectified supply voltages, can be seen, measured, and any distortions or hum content introduced can be localized in the exact part which is causing it. Once you use the scope on an electric organ, you will never be without it. Bias voltages can be calibrated from place to place, and even shorts are measurable.

Get a portable scope. Then, using the manual which comes with it, learn to do everything that the manufacturer suggests. Experiment on radios, even on the small voltages and waveforms from microphones, the output of phonograph cartridges, and the output of the speaker on your TV set. Make sure you get a multipurpose probe which is designed for high impedance circuits, so that is will not load down whatever circuit you touch. Calibrate the face of the scope voltage, learn to control vertical patterns and the horizontal spread on it, and you're ready to see your way through an organ.

It is a good idea to read carefully the manual illustrations on how waveform pictures are used in TV servicing. While in organ work you will be dealing with waveforms which may differ slightly in frequency from those the TV man watches, the principles upon which you troubleshoot with the scope are identical. You will learn how to analyze composite waveforms made up of two or more frequencies together. The organ will become a playfield for you with a scope. Nothing is hidden from you when you work with it. Little reasoning is required to locate the point at which a particular component is killing the organ signal.

For the more sophisticated technician, the scope offers a method of testing the characteristics of audio amplifiers and equipment better than any other. A square wave generator (basically that's what the Eccles-Jordan organ oscillator is) fed into an amplifier at 100 cycles per second or so will enable you to check out an amplifier and circuitry up to 1000 cycles per second. Once you reach a square wave frequency of 2000 cycles or so (also available from the organ oscillators) you can check out amplifier response up to maximum audible range.

The phase shift of an audio network can be checked by applying a sine wave to the circuit being tested and connecting a direct probe to the output terminal of the network. The signal is also fed into the scope through the H input and ground terminals. Set the H/sweep controls to H/in position. In the absence of phase shift, a sloping straight line will appear. Phase shift will show in an elliptical trace on the face of the scope. Frequency multiplication can be measured by the scope measure method, using the 60-cycles-per-second line frequency, which is available within the instrument.

Everyone associated with servicing electronic musical instruments should take a course in basic audio and oscillator theory and the use of the oscilloscope. With some intense practice, anyone can quickly learn to troubleshoot a complete electronic organ. While the author has never met an organ technician who used the scope for this purpose, it is time the idea was considered. In addition, with the advent of transistor circuitry, using a scope is the only way to make sure that what you are doing will not damage organ circuits in the process of looking for a malfunction. A scope may save you many hours of work.

The scope is recommended especially for the beginner in organ technology, because he will see theory put to work. It is recommended for the old line professional organ repairman because it makes the work easier and better in a day when everything seems to get more complicated.

The author fervently hopes that the instruction presented on these pages will not lead to argument over minor points. The author's intent is to broaden the knowledge of both the beginning piano technician and the experienced craftsman. No man learns alone; he learns by using ideas from others and implementing them with his own. The basics here are sound, and you alone can convert them into an art called piano technology.

Index

About the author . . . .

Rated a master craftsman among professional piano technicians, Dr. Stevens has been associated with the world of music almost all of his life. He teaches piano tuning and repair, is educational director of a guild, and operates shops in Ohio and Florida where he tunes, repairs, and rebuilds pianos. He is also an electronics expert, which serves him well in the repair of electronic pianos and organs.

Well known as a singer for many years, Dr. Stevens has given numerous concerts throughout the East and Middle West. He still composes and arranges music for his daughter, Sandra Lee, a professional organist.

Dr. Stevens began his musical studies at the Cincinnati Conservatory of Music, and continued through Ohio Northern University. He lived for a time in Great Britain, where he attended St. Andrew's College, and earned a Ph.D. at the Free Protestant University.

Dividing his time between Ohio and Florida, Dr. Stevens states that his Florida visits are not vacations, as he spends most of his time tuning and repairing pianos. "Fixing pianos is so pleasant and relaxing," he says, "that it's a vacation wherever you live!"

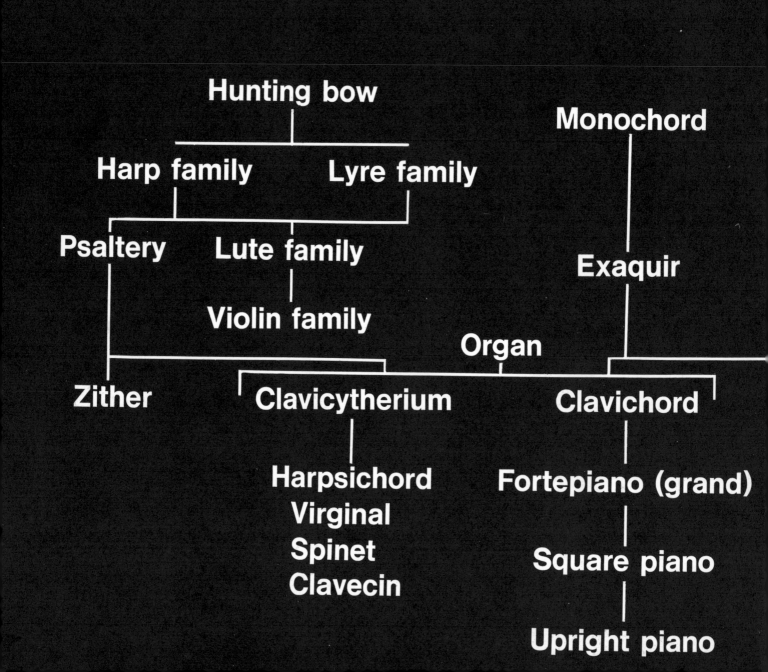